Put It In Writing

Fourth Edition

International Writing Institute, Inc., Cleveland, Ohio
Printed in the United States of America
ISBN: 0-911481-02-8

"There are no special kinds of writing . . ."

"You've got to look at it this way: There is only one English language, and the principles for using it effectively are the same, regardless the subject. In that sense, there are no special kinds of writing. If the subject is technical, it is technical writing. If the subject is medical, it is medical writing. The same for financial, or legal, or any other kind. There is just writing. And the things that make it easy to read and understand are the same—regardless the subject."

—From videotape discussion, Session 2

Technical Writing

THIS . . .

The equilibrium activity of the fission products as well as the induced activity from the isotopes observed, with the exception of W-187, indicated a linear relationship with reactor power level, and although the tungsten activity was higher than anticipated, it neither posed a safety problem nor caused any reactor operating difficulties. The varying manner of the tungsten activity levels in the coolant suggested that the cause in part was due to a non-uniform corrosive mechanism or that the total tungsten area exposed to a neutron flux varied during operation. Subsequent shutdown tests indicated that each of these conditions was indeed part of the release mechanism.

MEANS THIS:

The equilibrium activity of the fission products showed a linear relationship with power level. With the exception of W-187, the induced activity from the observed isotopes showed the same relationship. Although the tungsten activity was higher than expected, it did not pose a safety threat. Nor did it cause any reactor operating difficulties. The varying tungsten levels in the coolant suggested two possible causes: Either a non-uniform corrosion problem existed, or the total tungsten area exposed to a neutron flux varied during operation. Later tests confirmed that both these conditions existed.

DEVIL's ADVOCATE:
"But the lay reader still can't understand the right-hand versions."

Financial Writing

THIS . . .

Loan agreements requiring the Company and its subsidiaries to maintain a consolidated net working capital, as defined in the credit agreement of September 16, 1984, of not less than $8,000,000 and limiting dividends, except in capital stock of the Company, and stock payments subsequent to December 31, 1983 to the consolidated net income accumulated after that date plus $500,000 (approximately $2,061,000 unrestricted at December 31, 1985) necessitated long-term borrowing in the amount of $3,750,000 to correct the deficiency of approximately $350,000 in working capital as of December 31, 1985.

FOG Index 43
43rd grade in school

MEANS THIS:

The loan agreements call for two restrictions. They require the Company and its subsidiaries to maintain a consolidated net working capital, as defined in the credit agreement of September 16, 1984, of not less than $8,000,000. They also limit dividends, and stock payments after December 31, 1983, to the consolidated net income accumulated after that date plus $500,000. (This amount was approximately $2,061,000 unrestricted at December, 31, 1985.) Dividends in capital stock of the Company, however, are exempt from that limit. A deficiency of approximately $350,000 in working capital existed as of December 31, 1985. Long-term borrowing of $3,750,000 corrected this.

Index 12.2

Medical Writing

THIS . . .

Prior to admission the subject was ingesting NPH insulin, between 18 and 25 units on a daily basis, and on the initial day of admission was rehydrated through the utilization of forced fluids, normal saline with 5% dextrose and water, with subsequent augmentation of potassium supplement due to hypokalemia. On the above regimen the patient's condition improved and subsequent feeding initially included full liquids, subsequently 1500-calorie diabetic diet. The subject also during this admission experienced the aspiration of a thin bloody secretion via the nasogastric tube, indicated by a subsequent upper G.I. series to be associated with a sliding hiatus hernia without evidence of reflux or esophagitis.

MEANS THIS:

Before admission the patient was taking between 18 and 25 units of insulin daily. On the day of admission she was rehydrated with forced fluids, normal saline with 5% dextrose and water. Later we added potassium supplement to relieve hypokalemia. The patient's condition improved on this regimen, and we began feeding her full liquids, then a 1500-calorie diabetic diet. Also during this admission, the patient aspirated a thin bloody secretion through the nasogastric tube. An upper G.I. series showed a sliding hiatus hernia without evidence of reflux or esophagitis.

TEACHER: "But you usually aren't writing for lay readers. Engineers and scientists write to other engineers and scientists, and so on. If you must write for lay readers, then of course you must avoid (or define) words they don't know—if you care to be understood. That's the only difference."

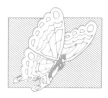

Contents

To the Participant:

This course has three major objectives: **Clarity, Speed, and Image.**

By the time the course is over you should be able to write more clearly—so clearly your reader cannot possibly misunderstand your message. You should be able to write faster—perhaps twice as fast in many cases—without wasting time fumbling over false starts and rewrites. And you should be able to present your valuable ideas in a way that pleases the reader and presents a pleasant, dignified image of you and your company.

Furthermore, you should achieve these goals with no sacrifice in the accuracy, dignity, or detail of **what** you write.

Your writing should also gain considerable beauty, if you care about that, for the same characteristics of language that make writing clear also give it beauty. In addition, this course should make you a better reader, speaker, and listener. Especially your reading should improve, for knowing how to recognize and analyze weaknesses in writing will surely help you overcome those weaknesses as you read.

The course is divided into two sections. In the first half, you will learn how to write more clearly. We will give you six principles of clear writing. We will explode some widespread taboos—bad advice about writing that you probably learned some time in your life. And we will give you a simple and famous formula by which you can measure how easy (or hard) your writing is to read.

The second half will deal with organizing. You will learn how to organize your reports and letters based on the reader's needs. You will learn how to get started, how to beat the deadline, how to avoid sexism, some special advice for letters, and how to review and edit the writing of others. We will also examine how computers can (and cannot) help in the writing process.

There are six sessions. The first part of each session—about one half hour—will be a televised presentation. That will be followed each time by about two hours of open discussion, questions, and review of your writing.

In this workbook you will find exercises on the most important points. Please do them. But also try after each session to apply the principles in your writing on the job **as soon as you can.** You should be able to notice improvement immediately after the first session.

There will be outside assignments. On each one, you will get an evaluation of your writing, pointing out your strengths and weaknesses. Also, these assignments will provide much of the discussion in your group after the videotape each session. We will show your writing to the group for analysis. That review of your own writing, and of the writing of your colleagues in the classroom, will provide an important part of your learning.

This workbook also contains a summary of the important material you will hear on the televised presentations. This is your permanent record; without it, we tend to forget very quickly what we hear. In the future, as you practice to improve your writing, plan to re-read the workbook periodically to reinforce the ideas in your mind. In this way, your learning will become complete and permanent.

ABOVE ALL, REMEMBER: Language is a transportation system for ideas—nothing more—a means to an end, not an end in itself. That is true whether you are writing a business report or the great American novel. Your purpose is to convey to your reader as much information as possible, as clearly and accurately as possible, in as little reading as possible. That is the only reason you write. It is the only reason cultures create language.

AJ
Cleveland, Ohio
1989

Part One
On Clarity

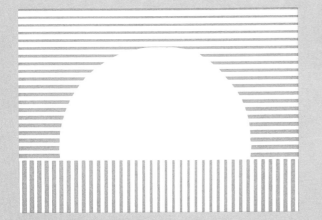

"The source of bad writing is the desire to be something more than a person of sense—the straining to be thought a genius. If people would only say what they have to say in plain terms, how much more eloquent they would be."

—Samuel Taylor Coleridge

Clarity–
Your First Objective

In any communication there is a sender and a receiver. The idea being communicated exists in the sender's brain as electricity, not words. If communication succeeds, that idea will end up in the receiver's brain as electricity. But we cannot transmit it that way, so we convert the idea from electricity to words. These are easy to transport, written or spoken. But they are just transportation.

The Major Problem

The first thing we ask of the language is *clarity*—that it transport your ideas clearly, accurately, and efficiently—so the message received is the one that was sent.

Of course, we can also paint beautiful word pictures with language, through literature and poetry. But that comes second. The only purpose for which cultures create language is to transport ideas. Then it is simple: We cannot afford a transportation system that damages its cargo in transit. The first objective of writing is clarity. **You have done your job as a writer, as the sender in the communications link, only when your ideas are so clear that your reader, the receiver, cannot possibly misunderstand them.**

Most people have a tendency to overcomplicate. Perhaps because they do not really know (nobody ever taught them) what makes good writing, they try to sound as scholarly as possible. In the process, they may destroy the ideas they are trying to transmit. This is a major problem in business, industry, and government agencies.

Here is an example of what can go wrong. This is what we mean when we say readers do not receive ideas accurately when you write in an overcomplicated or academic style. This is an actual piece of writing from the files of a government agency:

Technical assistance to institutional administrative staffs is authorized in determination of the availability and appropriate utilization of federal and state entitlements designating assistance in resolution of problems occasioned by requirements of handicapped children.

(33 words)

What does that say? We defy you to figure it out. Here is what the author meant:

> We can help your staff determine if federal or state funds are available to help meet the needs of handicapped children. We can also help you plan how best to use those funds.
>
> (33 words)

It is not likely that any reader would get that message, no matter how hard he or she worked at it. The transportation system has destroyed its cargo. The original passage may sound dazzling, but it does not communicate. An important idea is broadcast but not received.

That is not enough. Communication does not take place until the idea has been received accurately. And your job as a writer is to do whatever is necessary to be received accurately.

Speed

The second objective of this course is *speed*. Most people take far too long to write. That complicated style slows you down. As an example, just examine this passage from a company memo:

> from other cities in advance. All meetings will be in the conference room except Tuesday, June 28, which will be in the main cafeteria.
>
> **Management has become cognizant of the necessity for the elimination of undesirable vegetation surrounding the periphery of our facility.**
>
> (19 words)

Compare that with what the writer really wanted to say:

> from other cities in advance. All meetings will be in the conference room except Tuesday, June 28, which will be in the main cafeteria.
>
> **Please kill the weeds around the building.**
>
> (7 words)

We admit this example is exaggerated. But the overcomplicated style usually uses about twice as many words as necessary—sometimes even more. That means twice as many words you must put on paper. Whether you write them longhand, or dictate, or type your own, twice as many words means twice as long getting them recorded. Then consider this: *"Management has become cognizant of the necessity for the elimination of undesirable vegetation surrounding the periphery of our facility."* Those words do not come naturally. You must sit and wrestle with the words and with the sentence you will construct of them. This also slows you down.

But again, that meant *"Please kill the weeds around the building."* Those words come naturally; they are easy to write.

For those two reasons—because of the extra words and the extra time it takes to structure them—the unnecessarily complex style slows you down. Most intelligent adults should be able to write twice as fast as they do—perhaps even faster. That is the second objective of this course.

Image

Our final objective is that intangible we call *image*, or *leadership*, or *salesmanship*. Whether they should or not, people judge you all your life by the way you use your language, just as they judge you by the way you dress. More and more today, your contact with others is through writing. To influence others, you must first have valuable ideas. But that itself is not enough. The way you express those ideas will have much to do in determining whether your reader accepts them with confidence.

If your reader is your subordinate, we are describing an aspect of *leadership*. If he or she is your boss, it is *persuasiveness*. If you are writing to a customer, this same characteristic is an important part of *selling*.

Career advancement is at stake. It is no accident that the outstanding leaders in business and industry, government, the arts—in fact in all fields—are excellent communicators. That is how important writing is to your career. It is probably your second most important skill, regardless what field you are in. It is reasonable to assume that several times in your life your ability to write will make a difference in the advancement of your career.

Why People Write That Way

What causes people to write so often in that overcomplicated style we have described? Why is this Great American Windbag disease so widespread? You may write that way yourself. The odds favor it to some degree.

Honestly misguided. There are four common reasons for this bad habit. The first is quite innocent: *Most people write in that complex style because they honestly think it is the correct way to write.* Who can blame them? They see it all around them on the job. They have probably been encouraged to write that way in their universities, especially if they have done graduate study. They have also read so much that is hard to understand on the job and in their professional journals. Who can blame you for just gradually getting the idea: "This is the way I'm supposed to write."

But the second, third, and fourth reasons for this heavy style are not so innocent.

The Penguin Joke

A truck delivering a load of penguins broke down on the way to the zoo. The day was hot, and the driver was aware that his precious cargo could not last long without air conditioning. He ran to the street, flagged down the first empty truck that passed, explained the emergency to the other driver, and quickly transferred the little darlings to the good truck. Then he handed the other driver fifty dollars and instructed: "Take these penguins to the zoo."

Later, his truck fixed, the first driver headed back to the garage. As he passed an amusement park, he saw penguins everywhere. Penguins on the carousel, penguins on the roller coaster, penguins standing in line for popcorn. He slammed on the brakes, ran into the park and found the other driver, shook him by the lapels, and yelled: "I told you to take them to the zoo! I gave you fifty dollars and said, 'Take these penguins to the zoo!'"

And the other guy said: "I did. And we had money left over, so I brought 'em here."

Moral: No matter how clear you try to be, someone will find a way to misunderstand. (And if you don't try, everyone will.)

(Also see: *The Hippopotamus Joke*, page 91.)

Most style manuals agree with this simple rule: Spell out one-digit numbers (one through nine), and use numerals for any number having two or more digits.

There are some exceptions, but they are logical and simple. Use numerals for all numbers in dates and street addresses, and for numbering consecutive items (such as paragraph numbers), no matter how high or low.

Also, use numerals for *all* numbers in a sentence if it contains both kinds (209 applicants for 5 jobs). The idea here is to be consistent within any sentence, to avoid confusing readers.

Lazy thinking. The second reason overcomplicated writing is so widespread is: *The writer has not thought out his or her ideas clearly enough.* After all, writing is the end result of your thinking, on paper. That is basic. But if you accept this, you must also accept that the writing cannot possibly be any clearer than the thinking.

Unfortunately, when writers use difficult language, it is possible to express ideas that are only half thought out, yet in a way that sounds dazzlingly scholarly. In fact, it is easy. We repeat because this point is so important: *You cannot express an idea in ultimate simplicity until you have thought it out in ultimate simplicity.*

Trying to impress. The third reason for heavy writing is: *trying to impress others.* The type of person guilty of this usually is a little unsure of his or her ideas, or perhaps unsure of what the boss thinks of him or her. Rather pathetically, this person is begging through the writing: "Please, won't someone notice how intelligent I am?"

Impress others with your writing, by all means. But follow the example of professional writers—impress with the value of *what* you write, not the scholarly sound of *how* you write it. Let the impressiveness, the scholarliness, the dignity and beauty of your writing come from the *ideas* you express, not the *words and sentences* with which you express them. You will do more impressing this way. After all, you are past the point in life when you could impress people with the size of your vocabulary.

Concealing weak material. The fourth reason writers prefer unnecessarily complex style is fraud: *to conceal weak material.* The writer knows the ideas are weak and hopes deliberately to cover this up. He or she hopes that if the work can be made to sound so complicated nobody can understand it, nobody will recognize it has said very little.

Unfortunately, it is quite easy for writers to succeed with this kind of deception, because large words often conceal that the ideas are not thought out very precisely. Furthermore, most readers have profound respect for things they cannot understand. They would be embarrassed to admit they cannot understand them.

Sometimes it appears the whole world is playing a sort of literary version of "The Emperor's New Clothes." Few people can understand much of what is written. But nobody will admit it.

ALWAYS REMEMBER. Whenever you write, you are dealing with two different factors: your ideas (WHAT you write) and the language used to convey them (HOW you write). Although they are related, they are totally separate considerations. This course deals only with the HOW.

Six Principles of Clear Writing

These principles will be the basis of the first half of this course. They apply to all kinds of writing; they are not just principles of business writing or engineering writing. They would be equally appropriate if you were to try to write a newspaper article or the great American novel.

The Six Principles are:

- Prefer clear, familiar words.
- Keep most sentences short and simple.
- Prefer active voice verbs; avoid passives.
- Get people into your writing.
- Use a conversational style.
- Gather all your information before you start writing.

In this session we will examine Principles One and Two in detail. Next session the other four will be discussed.

Principle 1:

Prefer Clear, Familiar Words

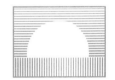

Have you ever stopped to think about the purpose of vocabulary? Your objectives in choosing words should be clarity and precision.

There can be no question that small words are usually the clearest, easiest to understand. This is easy to prove statistically. When we say prefer clear, familiar words, this does not mean never use a large word. Rather, do not use a large word when you can say exactly the same thing with a small one. When you do, you are increasing the communications line resistance unnecessarily between sender and receiver. Smart writers will do nothing to increase that line resistance unnecessarily.

Small words are usually more precise. You may be surprised to learn that large words are usually *less precise* than small ones. (You will see examples as this course progresses.) Remember, the objective is to be clear and precise—at the receiving end.

Do not use *'facilitate'* when you could say *'help.'* Do not use *'utilize'* when you could say *'use,'* or *'endeavor'* when you could say *'try,'* or *'sufficient'* when you could say *'enough.'* Do not use a word like *'subsequently'* when you could say— well, as a matter of fact, what would you say instead?

'Subsequently' is an example of how large words can create misunderstanding. It is an interesting example of what we mean when we say large words are usually less precise than small ones. Ask people what 'subsequently' means, and you are likely to get three different responses: *'next,' 'later,'* or *'therefore.'* As a matter of fact, *'subsequently'* can mean *'next'* or *'later.'* And, even though they are incorrect, many writers use it to mean *'therefore,'* and many readers read it that way. Of course, the writer knows which of those three meanings he or she intends. But the reader has no way of knowing. Imprecision is introduced through a word larger than necessary.

Another such word is *'parameters'*—a favorite of engineers and scientists. Even dictionaries disagree what it means, and most people who use it intend it to mean *'limits.'* This is a fancy misuse of *'perimeters.'*

Or, consider the word *'indicated'*—another favorite. Does the writer mean *'proved'* or *'suggested'*? The reader cannot tell. Remember, readers are paper readers, not mind readers.

Your attitude toward choice of words is a major factor in determining how clear your writing will be. Granted, *'sufficient'* is not much harder to read than *'enough.'* But it is an unnecessary overload, no matter how slight. If your attitude is to choose words harder than needed, you may do that several times every sentence—perhaps 30 or 40 times on a page. The collective load to the reader is devastating, as in this short example:

Solicit the employee's assistance in achieving resolution of the problem.

That means:

Ask the employee's help in solving the problem.

Imagine the burden of reading sentence after sentence, paragraph after paragraph, written in the unnecessarily heavy style of the first example above. Readers would not have much hope of receiving much information.

You will certainly need some large words. Simply do not use them when you can say the same thing with small words. The large words you will probably need will be the vocabulary of your profession. Interestingly, they usually express ideas new to society. If you were a chemist, for example, you would certainly need a term like *'polymerization.'* An engineer needs *'magnetohydrodynamics.'* An accountant needs words like *'liquidation,'* *'profitability,'* *'depreciable.'* There are no small words to express these concepts.

Similarly, the medical profession needs specialized words like *'hemodialysis.'* But *'epistaxis'* complicates unnecessarily; it means *'nosebleed,'* and that is what doctors should call it.

Develop a large vocabulary, by all means. But use it graciously. Do not show off with it. Have the large words available when you need them, but you should not need most of them very often.

Remember, even though you may know the large words, your reader may not. And remember, your job is not just to broadcast, but *to be received*. You, the broadcaster, must do whatever is necessary to be received accurately. Anything less than that would be intellectually snobbish, and unrealistic.

Small words add beauty. Another misguided argument is that *beauty* in writing comes from large words. No, no. Large words may sometimes offer you the opportunity to say something complicated that you could not express in small words. But certainly you cannot argue that they add beauty. As a matter of fact, the large words are usually the ones that *take away* the beauty from the language. People who use them sound like a government report on the price of cabbages. There is not much beauty in that kind of 'officialese' writing. And such writers all sound alike, so large words also tend to destroy individual style in writing.

In words, the factors that contribute most to beauty are imagery and rhythm. Surely imagery is greater in small words: *joy in the eyes of a child . . . the smell of fresh cut grass . . . .* And rhythm is far easier to control with small words. These are the reasons poets rely on them almost entirely.

Do Not Use	When You Could Say:	Do Not Use	When You Could Say:
accordingly	therefore; so	indebtedness	debt
aforementioned	these	indicate	show
applicable	apply to	in order to	to
assistance	aid; help	in the event that	if
attributable	due	in the near future	soon
by means of	by	prior to	before
compensate	pay	provided that	if
consequently	so	purchase	buy
considerable	much	terminate	end
correspondence	letter	transmit	send
facilitate	help; ease	utilize	use
foregoing	this; these	visualize	see
furthermore	also	whether or not	whether
inasmuch as	because	with regard to	about

Some commonly used words that are harder than necessary, and simpler substitutes.

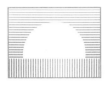

Principle 2:

Keep Most Sentences Short and Simple

From our observations of thousands of adults in business and government, this is the help you probably need most. **You should be averaging 15 to 20 words per sentence.** If you are like most business people, you are probably averaging in the mid- or upper twenties.

Remember, we say you should *average* between 15 and 20 words per sentence. Mix them up. The shortest possible sentence in the English language is two words: subject and verb. There is no maximum.

A good sentence can run quite long. The trouble is, you probably cannot write long sentences very well unless you have the skill of a professional writer. Most people risk grammatical errors at about 30 or 35 words. At that length, it becomes more likely that you will make a grammatical mistake than that you will not.

Long sentences are hard to read. Like unnecessarily hard words, they increase the communications line resistance between writer and reader. Even if you can write long sentences and keep the grammar correct, they are likely to do a poor job of transmitting your ideas. Your reader may get tangled, unable to follow each idea from beginning to end. Of course, it will almost always look clear to you, the writer. But remember: You, the writer, have one major advantage your reader will never have. *You know what you are trying to say.* You are not relying on those black marks on the page to find out.

One major idea to a sentence. Long sentences often contain two or more ideas, and that is a violation of the *second half* of Principle Two: Keep Most Sentences Short *AND SIMPLE.* By '*simple,*' we mean that each sentence should be devoted to only one major idea.

When you put two major ideas into one sentence, as you tend to do in long sentences, you risk grammatical errors. Examine this sentence:

Hon. H. H. St. Jacques
Commissioner
U.S. Interstate Commerce Commission
Washington, D.C. 20019

Dear Commissioner,

Thank you for your letter of December 18. As you requested, we are enclosing a copy of the Ex Parte 813 proposal. This is the examiner's final recommendation, quite different from your earlier study, which badly upset our client.

We do not agree with the Commission on this interpretation, and plan to introduce new tariff. . . .

That is not a very long sentence—just 17 words. But it violates the second half of Principle Two, keeping major ideas in separate sentences. Of course, the flaw is obvious. Did the recommendation or the study upset the client? If you are to figure out which one it was, you must do so through rules of grammar or punctuation. However, a reader is not likely to work that hard. In fact, a reader is not likely to notice two different meanings are possible in a sentence like that one. The reader will react subconsciously, thinking either the department's recommendation or the earlier study upset the client, unaware the statement could be read either way.

If, as you read that passage, you thought *the study* upset the client, it was probably because you reacted subconsciously to a rule of grammar you learned in 8th or 9th grade—*the rule of pronoun antecedents.* That rule says a pronoun will try to stand for the last noun before it. The pronoun is *'which.'* And what is the last noun that appears before it? *'Study.'* Therefore, grammar tells us *the study* upset the client.

But if you thought *the department's recommendation* upset the client, you have grammar on your side too—*the rule of nonrestrictive clauses and phrases.* This rule tells us we can lift out the part between the commas and read the sentence without it. Then the sentence reads: *"This is the examiner's final recommendation, which badly upset our client."*

So, grammar tells you either meaning can be correct. Your response as a reader of that sentence would depend on which rule of grammar you happen to react to subconsciously.

The writer made that mistake because he or she tried to put two major ideas into one grammatical structure, and they would not quite fit. That is a common mistake. The longer the sentence, the more likely that you will make some grammar error.

You may be thinking, "Not me. I'm good enough to write long sentences and keep the grammar straight." Perhaps you are. But your reader still may not understand you. After all, grammatically correct does not mean clear.

Short sentences are easier to write. Have you ever found yourself stuck while writing? Not stuck getting started; that is an organizing problem, and we will talk about it in the second half of this course. Rather, stuck in the middle of the writing. Then ask yourself, "Where am I stuck?" At precisely what point in the writing?

Notice carefully the next time this happens. You will probably find you are stuck in the middle of a sentence. You can always start one; but finishing some of them may give you fits. When you are stuck, the structure is probably wrong. Probably you have too many ideas in that sentence, and the grammar will not fit them all.

How do you get unstuck? You probably stagger desperately to the next period to get out of that mess. But that is all wrong. You are leaving the mess behind for the reader to clean up. When you are stuck in the middle of a sentence, do not stagger on. Rather, retreat to the last period and start again. Separate that long sentence into two, three, or four short ones. You will soon be unstuck, able to say what you want with little trouble.

This should save you much time. Just by building sentences easily *and naturally,* you can probably write much faster than you do. It is those long, awkward sentences that slow you down so much.

Instant help: The Meat Cleaver Technique. Another suggestion from professional writers is the *'meat cleaver technique.'* Often you can help a long sentence greatly by simply chopping it into two shorter ones. This is possible when the sentence contains two major ideas, one after the other.

Chop the long sentence neatly in two. Sometimes doing so is as easy as changing a comma to a period and beginning the second half with a capital letter. Sometimes it may be necessary to cauterize the wound—change a few words to restore proper grammar after the chop.

Infamous Quotation No. 1

In 1977 President Jimmy Carter issued an order requiring all federal regulations in plain English. The implications were awesome, and there were strong reactions (mostly negative) throughout the government.

In June 1978 at the Brookings Institution, a group of legal scholars, writing experts, and government executives met to discuss the implications of the President's order. At this meeting, a dean of the Columbia University School of Law said: "I'm not sure I'm comfortable with the idea of legal writing in plain English. The whole thing seems sort of anti-intellectual to me."

(Also see: *On Legal Writing,* page 62.)

(Also see: *Infamous Quotation No. 2,* page 87.)

You need not always divide separate ideas into separate sentences. If the two major ideas are short, they will not overburden the reader as one sentence. But if that sentence gets very long, more than 25 or 30 words, it probably will overburden the reader. Chop it in two. This is probably the easiest and most immediate way of improving your writing—and saving much of that time we promised earlier.

Here you see an example of that *'meat cleaver technique'* and how it makes the writing clearer. First, the original:

The Shore Engineering District has requested the installation of an additional terminal at 18419 River Road for the purpose of providing access to the General Electric time sharing computer system.

Here is the logical breaking point:

The Shore Engineering District has requested the installation of an additional terminal at 18419 River Road ● for the purpose of providing access to the General Electric time sharing computer system.

This is what the *'meat cleaver technique'* can do. Notice that in this example it was necessary to do a little rewording at the chop:

The Shore Engineering District has requested the installation of an additional terminal at 18419 River Road. Its purpose will be to provide access to the General Electric time sharing computer system.

Long sentences may bury ideas. When we recommend one major idea to a sentence, this does not mean we are ruling out subordinate clauses. Rather, it means you should use subordinate clauses only for subordinate ideas. Subordinate means *less important*. Do not put two *major* ideas in the same sentence. Even if you can keep the grammar straight, you end up with buried ideas. They are likely to compete for emphasis, for the reader's attention. One wins, and the other loses. Or they share equally, and neither idea gets the attention it deserves.

Here is an example of a major idea buried as a subordinate clause. The buried part is between the commas:

Your automobile policy, which would still cost $82.50 if you had not moved to a new address, went up in cost this year because your bank required that you add comprehensive and collision coverage.

Here is the same thing rewritten as two sentences, with that buried idea getting full emphasis:

Your automobile policy went up in cost this year because your bank required that you add comprehensive and collision coverage. It would still cost $82.50 if you had not moved to a new address.

THE PERIOD IS THE NOBLEST PUNCTUATION MARK OF THEM ALL—and the most overlooked. Generally, it is safe to say: The more periods your writing contains, the better it will be. But there is a danger in overchopping—in shortening sentences too much. Your writing might sound like 'Run, Spot, run. See Spot run.' It might sound choppy, childish. Worse, the sentences would probably not be tailored for the ideas. But 'Run, Spot, run. See Spot run.' averages three words per sentence. We said your writing should average between 15 and 20. If it does, it should sound neither choppy nor childish.

INTERNATIONAL WRITING INSTITUTE, INCORPORATED
HANNA BUILDING. CLEVELAND. OHIO 44115-1993 TELEPHONE 216•696-4032

12 words
23

3

35

Good writing almost always averages between 15 and 20 words per sentence. Do not write all sentences within these limits, however, because doing so would make your style so dull it would bore your reader. Mix them up. Although probably not aware of it, your reader feels comfortable with the changing pace people experience when the sentences are occasionally as short as 3 or 4 words or as long as 30 or 35.

9

27

There are reasons your favorite authors are your favorites. Skilled writers do many things with language to create exactly the mood they want, and one of the most effective of these is control of sentence length.

12
7

12
23

Short sentences give emphasis; the shorter one is, the harder it hits. They also create the feeling of action. This is because shorter sentences mean more sentences and therefore more verbs. Verbs are the action words, and so skilled writers deliberately use short sentences to create the tense, fast-moving mood appropriate for action passages.

25

35

25

Long sentences, on the other hand, are generally useful for the slower pace necessary in descriptive passages, as important for proper balance as the action. They meander along, like peaceful stretches of a river, at the relaxed speed best suited for detailed viewing, slowly, deliberately unfolding information about the people, places, and things that provide the background for the actions. Although an important part of most writing, these passages tend to subordinate the ideas they contain and therefore are generally ineffective for presenting major ideas.

19
―――
267

It is the combination of these two techniques that causes readers to say, "I couldn't put the book down."

The shortest sentence in this passage is 3 words, and the longest is 35. The average is a very readable 19 words per sentence.

Review

How alert were you? All of these important points were discussed in the videotaped presentation you just watched. You should be able to answer them all. If you cannot, look them up in this book.

Please list the three major benefits of good writing, which are also the objectives of this course.

Clarity

Speed

Image

What are the four common reasons intelligent adults write in a heavy style?

Honestly misguided

Lazy thinking

Trying to impress

Concealing weak material

What are the two separate factors you always deal with when writing?

What you write

how you write

What three major advantages do small words have over large ones?

Clearest / easiest to understand

more precise

add beauty / imagery / rythym

What are the disadvantages of long sentences? (Four were mentioned in the text; you may be able to add others.)

hard to read

risk grammatical error

they bury ideas

harder to write

longer to write

What should be the average number of words per sentence? *15 to 20*

It is desirable for **all** sentences to be that length. True or false? *false*

PRACTICE
Small words add
clarity and beauty.

SESSION 1
Exercises

EXERCISE 1.

Opposite each word or group of words below, write a word that better says the same thing. (For some, you may need a few words):

	Your word:	Course recommends:
Detrimental	harmful	HARMFUL
Simultaneously	At the same time →	
Sufficient	Enough →	
Consequently	Therefore / so → *As a result*	
Possesses	Has	HAS
Capability	ability →	
Numerous	Many →	
Punctual	On time →	
Molecular	Molecular →	
Endeavor	DO	Try
Verification	Check	Proof
Concur	Agree	Agree
Deferral	Delay	Delay
Accelerate	speed up →	
In close proximity	Near →	
Take cognizance of	Recognize	Recognize
At the present time	Now →	
In the event that	If →	
Due to the fact that	Because of →	
Maximum quantity	top number	Most
Minimum quantity	smallest amt.	least
Termination	End	End
Excessive	too much →	

EXERCISE 2.

Large words often make writing unclear. By obscuring ideas, they sometimes fail to communicate, as in this example:

Our inability to approve your application for credit is based on insufficient down payment. We are concerned with the potential inability to meet repayment obligations as scheduled due to inadequate income.

Your Rewrite

Due to your lack of down payment, we are unable to approve your application for credit. we are concerned that Your income is not ~~adeq~~ enough to meet the payment Schedule.

Course Recommends

We can not approve your loan with such a low down payment. You might not be able to afford the monthly payments.

EXERCISE 3.

Large words may make your writing sound cold, robbing it of charm. Try rewriting this passage:

Mr. McWayte addressed this office's May staff meeting. Attendees were duly impressed with the multitudinous tasks involved in the accumulation of relevant, pertinent data and how these tasks are implemented by the MCS staff.

Your Rewrite

~~The May~~ Mr. McWayte spoke to the staff members at the May meeting. The members present were impressed with the ~~presentation~~. ~~It~~ many tasks needed in gathering the important data and how the MCS staff performs them.

Course Recommends

EXERCISE 4.

Try to make this long sentence clearer and its ideas stronger by chopping it into two or more shorter ones (the meat cleaver technique):

Roman, ~~who~~ throws a 95-mph fastball and has a changeup and good slider, suffered his worst defeat since he was named rookie of the year two seasons ago, allowing a one-out single to Rod Brewer in the first then walking three straight batters, throwing ten straight balls at one point.

Your Rewrite

_____

_____

_____

_____

_____

_____

_____

_____

_____

_____

Course Recommends

_____

_____

_____

_____

_____

_____

_____

PRACTICE
Short sentences are easier to write.

EXERCISE 5.

This one requires more than just chopping. You will have to simplify some words as well:

This kind of action should be formal and direct, involving ~~thorough~~ analysis of all ~~pertinent~~ factors and presentation of a wide range of specific alternatives~~such that~~the GW supervisor merely has to choose from an array of facts which by ~~their mere presence~~ instills confidence and assurance that GW employees are getting the best benefits program that is available.

(handwritten annotations: complete, important)

(By the way, did you notice the grammatical error? Errors of this kind become more likely as the sentence gets longer.)

Your Rewrite

This "kind of" action should be formal and direct, involving analysis of important factors and presenting alternatives. The G.W. Supervisor must choose

You must study all related factor and present a wide range of choices

Course Recommends

EXERCISE 6. (optional)

Even financial or legal statements, which so often baffle readers, can be thoroughly readable. The passage below can be improved greatly just by breaking two monstrously long sentences into several shorter ones. But you can improve it still further by using easier words and trimming wasted words:

The attached Statement of Consolidated Income for the six months ended June 30, 1985 and June 30, 1984 for the Standard Chair Company (a Michigan corporation) and consolidated subsidiary companies has been prepared in accordance with accepted accounting principles from the books of the companies.

Pursuant to Section 5.1 of the Note Agreement dated June 15, 1985 providing for the issuance and sale by the Standard Chair Company of $50,000,000 aggregate principal amount of 9.55% notes due July 15, 2010, the undersigned, an authorized officer, does hereby certify that, to the best of my knowledge, the Standard Chair Company has performed and observed all of, and is not at the date hereof in default in the performance or observance of any of the terms, provisions, or conditions of said Note Agreement and that there exists no Event of Default, as defined by Section 9.1 of same.

Your Rewrite

_____

_____

_____

_____

_____

_____

_____

_____

_____

_____

_____

_____

_____

_____

_____

(Continued on next page)

EXERCISE 6 Your rewrite (continued):

_____

_____

_____

_____

**Course
Recommends**

_____

_____

_____

_____

_____

_____

_____

_____

_____

_____

_____

_____

_____

_____

_____

_____

_____

_____

Notes

- Thinking is the art of simplifying ideas

- Technical Writing
  1.) Product of writer who understands subject
  2.) Focuses on subject only
  3.) Conveys one meaning

"The first human being who hurled a curse instead of a weapon against his adversary was the founder of civilization."

—Sigmund Freud

Changing Some Old Attitudes

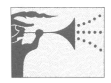

Remember, it is possible to express even your most difficult ideas clearly and simply, *with no sacrifice of accuracy*. While achieving a style that is clear and easy to read, you will also be adding beauty and dignity to your writing.

Session One introduced you to the two most important principles of clarity: familiar words and easy sentences. Here, now, are the other four of the Six Principles of Clear Writing:

Prefer active voice verbs; avoid passives.
Get people into your writing.
Use a conversational style.
Gather all your information before you start writing.

This session, we will also examine why the advice in this course may disagree with some of what you have learned before, and we will explode some old taboos about language and writing. We will also consider the roles of brevity and courtesy in your writing.

Principle 3:

Prefer Active Voice Verbs; Avoid Passives

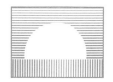

When you were learning the basics of sentence structure in the 8th or 9th grade, your English teacher probably taught you some sentence like, *"The dog buried the bone."* And you learned those basic terms—subject, transitive verb, direct object. (Dog - buried - bone.)

That sentence structure is the backbone of the English language. It is in the ACTIVE voice. The same thing in the passive voice would be, *"The bone was buried by the dog."*

The danger. In your writing you might say, *"The customer approved the plans."* That is the same structure as *"The dog buried the bone."* Subject, transitive verb, direct object. (Customer - approved - plans.)

In the passive voice that statement would be, *"The plans were approved by the customer."* Notice in the passive voice the subject is *'plans.'* The verb is still *'approved,'* but it has picked up the auxiliary *'were.'* And the object now is *'customer.'* Subject and object have traded places.

In the active voice, which is the more natural way, the subject performs the action and the object receives it. In the passive, instead of performing the action, the subject receives the action of the verb. The passive voice does not need an object. In fact, the object hangs there rather awkwardly. Notice it is no longer the direct object of a transitive verb; rather, it has become the indirect object of the preposition *'by.'*

But the entire prepositional phrase is an unnecessary part of the grammar. Because it hangs there awkwardly, you are tempted to drop it out. When you do, the sentence reads, *"The plans were approved."* **The passive voice does not tell by whom, and that is usually an important part of the information.** You see how important it is in these two samples:

The following procedure <u>is recommended</u>:

　When the red light <u>goes</u> on, the instrument <u>should be shut</u> down and all settings <u>should be checked</u>. It <u>should be turned</u> on again only when it <u>is confirmed</u> that all pressures are within tolerances.

Notice how much more information the active voice conveys:

The <u>union recommends</u> the following procedure:

　When the red light <u>goes</u> on, the <u>operator should shut</u> the instrument down and the <u>supervisor should check</u> all settings. The <u>lab assistant should turn</u> it on again only when the <u>research manager confirms</u> that all pressures are within tolerances.

At no time is a passive as risky as when you are writing procedures, or other written instructions. Do not write, *"The statement must be updated every three months . . . ."* The work might not get done. You are saying something must be done but not who must do it. The reader may not realize he or she is supposed to do it. Rather write, *"You must update the statement every three months . . . ."* (or whoever else). Notice the difference? The active voice is clearer and more emphatic, and therefore the instructions are more likely to be followed.

The passive is not always wrong. Sometimes *by whom* is obvious or not important. For example, in a research report a scientist is usually describing his or her own work. *By whom* is obvious. And if he or she were to report that work in the active voice the subject would repeatedly be *'I.'* That would be inappropriate. In this case the passive would probably be better. But even when the passive does not conceal information, it risks making the writing dull. Therefore, careful writers should use it sparingly.

Caution: *'passive'* and *'past'* are not the same. They sound somewhat alike only by accident. Do not assume that all passive voice verbs are in the past tense. Passives occur in all tenses. We could say, *'The plans were approved.'* . . . *'The plans are being approved.'* . . . or *'The plans will be approved.'* There you have past, present, and future tenses. But they are all passive, and all equally poor for the same reason.

Passives are easy to recognize. They all have some form of the verb '*to be*' in front of the main verb. "*The proposal **was** approved.*" "*The statement **must be** updated.*" After you have recognized it, turning it active is simple. Just ask yourself 'By whom?' The answer to that question gives you the subject you need for an active voice sentence.

"*It is recommended that we make the changes.*" By whom? "*The Atlanta office recommends that we make the changes.*" Or, "*I recommend that we make the changes.*" "*Mary is loved.*" By whom? John? Her mother? All the boys at the pool hall? You see, '*by whom*' can make a great difference to your reader.

Principle 4:

Get People Into Your Writing

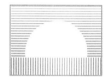

There is a widespread superstition that good business writing must be impersonal. Misguided writers have even coined a name for this style. '*Third person*' style, you call it. But you really mean '*no person.*' And that is silly, sometimes even harmful.

Why do people write in this impersonal style? Usually they do not know. The answer usually given is "*Well, we've always done it that way.*" An inadequate explanation. Or, some people argue that the writing is more likely to be objective if it is impersonal. But when you stop and think about it, why would it be?

People are often an important part of what you are writing about. Why try to hide it? By all means refer to them in your writing.

This does not mean pulling people in artificially. Rather, do not go out of your way to keep them out of your writing. Refer to people and companies by their names. Certainly you may call people '*he,*' '*she,*' or '*they.*' In fact, you may even call yourself '*I.*' There is absolutely no restriction against this—with one sensible limitation: Your English teachers probably told you, "Don't repeat *I, I, I,* over and over again." They were right. But an occasional '*I*' is perfectly proper—even in the most serious and dignified writing.

You are certainly no better off referring to yourself as '*the writer*' or '*the undersigned.*' Those are just stuffy, old-fashioned synonyms for '*I.*' And if there are any objections to '*I,*' those objections must certainly apply to '*the writer*' or '*the undersigned*' as well.

But caution: Do not use '*I*' and '*we*' interchangeably; that would be inappropriate. Use '*I*' when referring to yourself and '*we*' when referring to your company. When you are in doubt, '*we*' is probably appropriate.

Generally, referring to people will make your writing sound more courteous and pleasant. Of greater importance, the writing will be more informative and precise.

Principle 5:

Use a Conversational Style

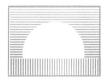

If we could give you just one piece of advice, it would be this. Principle Five tends to force you to do all the others correctly.

When we say '**Use a conversational style,**' this does not mean to write in slang or in a careless way. Writing should be more precise than conversation, because in writing both the writer and reader have more time. You can be—and should be—more careful. The reader expects it. He or she will ignore some carelessness in your talking, but will not forgive that same carelessness in your writing.

Most people are far better talkers than writers. (Except, of course, for formal speeches. Then they do exactly the same things wrong that they do in writing. And for the same reasons. In fact, they usually write the speech. No wonder there are so many deadly speeches.)

There are two main reasons you probably communicate better talking than writing. First, you have had more experience talking. Most people started talking at about age two and have rarely shut up since. And second, you get instant feedback in conversation. That is important. When you are face-to-face with your receiver, you have many ways of knowing whether you have communicated successfully. Even though you may not have been aware it was happening, that instant feedback has helped you improve your talking skills all of your life.

As a result, most people have those two distinct personalities when they communicate. The difference is so pronounced it is almost as though there were a switch in the back of the head, with one position for talking and the other for writing. The purpose of Principle Five, then, is to get you to write with your switch in the talking position. But it may not be easy.

Here is another tip from the professional writers. **When you are having trouble finding just the right approach to express an idea, ask yourself: "How would I say this to a loved one or friend at dinner tonight?"** It may not be easy, but if you can force yourself to imagine how you would express an idea to someone in relaxed conversation, away from the job, that is close to the best way to write it.

No doubt you can remember reading something you could not understand. So you asked the writer, who replied: "What I mean is . . . ."—then went on to tell you what it meant in simple, precise English. You then answered, "Oh, I see." And you probably muttered to yourself: "Why didn't you write it that way in the first place?" He or she probably should have.

Again, that warning, however. Most of us are a bit careless when we talk. **You must be more careful to be grammatically correct in writing than in talking.** But that should not be hard. You will probably have no trouble using correct grammar if you do not try to use long and complicated sentences. The true Principle Five, then, should probably read: *"Use a conversational style; well, sort of, anyhow."*

Principle 6:
Gather All Your Information Before You Start Writing

This advice is not about *organizing* your writing. That comes in the second half of the course. Rather, we are still discussing your ability to express yourself clearly and accurately. In the introduction of this course, we established that writing is your thinking on paper, and therefore the writing cannot possibly be any clearer than the thinking.

It is this simple: You cannot *write* an idea clearly until you have *thought it out* clearly, and you cannot *think it out* clearly until you have all of the information necessary to do so.

Some writers start too soon. Ironically, they are usually the most conscientious workers—the ones who do not like to leave major jobs for the last minute. They start writing the report early in the project. Certainly you should keep detailed notes from the beginning of any project. But do not start the finished writing until you have all of the information you need for the clear *thinking* that clear writing demands. That is usually at the end of the project.

Furthermore, something else marvelous happens when you have gathered all of the information in advance. Your confidence level goes up, so your tendency toward heavy language goes down. Remember, to express yourself well, you must be confident that your IDEAS will do the necessary impressing. For that kind of confidence, you must be able to sit down to write with the attitude, "I *know* my subject, and I *know* that I know my subject." But you usually cannot say that until you have finished gathering the information.

The Three Taboos

At this point, you may be thinking that some of the advice in this course sounds the opposite of what you have learned before. You are entitled to some explanation.

Unfortunately, most people never learn to write in school. That is amazing, because throughout your education you probably spent more time studying English than any other subject. But for the most part you studied literature. Perhaps the teachers hoped that somehow you would learn how to write by observing how others wrote. They probably gave you very little specific advice.

Worse, some may have given you **bad** advice. Has any teacher ever encouraged you to use the largest words you can, or to write very long sentences? Again, the influence may have been literature. What the teacher did not tell you, however, is that the English language has changed drastically since much of the English language's great literature was written. (For example: In Shakespeare's "Romeo, Romeo, wherefore art thou Romeo?" Juliet is not asking, *Where are you, Romeo;* she is asking *Why are you Romeo*—a bit of self-pity. *Wherefore* was the common word in Elizabethan England for *why,* and that is typical of the changes which have altered English through the centuries.) Gradually, much of literature became so hard to understand that English teachers had to become specialists at explaining it. They still are. And many still hold literary style up as the example of how you should write today.

Still, here and there you probably learned some rules. Many of them are helpful. But unfortunately, most people also learned some harmful pieces of advice.

These are usually negative—things you were told you may not do. Three in particular are so widespread almost everybody has been exposed to them. You probably learned them as rules of grammar, or rules of composition. But these three are not rules and never have been. Let us expose them and get rid of them forever.

TABOO NO. 1—*THAT YOU MAY NOT BEGIN SENTENCES WITH 'AND' or 'BUT.'* Of course you may. In fact, there are times you should. Here is why:

Can you remember what we call these words? What part of speech? They are conjunctions, or *'connectives.'* What do they connect? Your ideas. And what is the basic vehicle of the idea? *The sentence.* When the English teacher tells you that you may not begin sentences with *'And'* or *'But,'* you are deprived of the two most useful words for connecting sentences smoothly. Two choices remain: You may have the smooth flow of the connective, **or** the clarity and efficiency of short sentences, but you may not have both.

But good writers refuse to make that choice. What can be wrong with short smooth sentences? **Connectives allow you smooth, logical flow from sentence to sentence AND the clarity and impact of short sentences.**

Of course, do not go out of your way to begin sentences with *'And'* or *'But.'* Rather, do not back off from doing so when it seems the natural thing to do. Here is an example in which a splendid writer felt it was natural and desirable to begin sentences with *'And'* and *'But.'* *The Wall Street Journal* is regularly one of the best written publications in the United States:

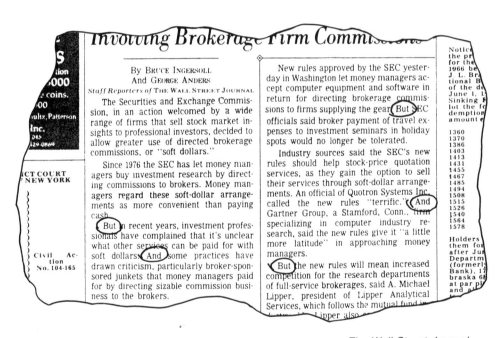

—The Wall Street Journal

You may be thinking, *"The Wall Street Journal* has literary freedom to bend the rules of grammar." But we are not teaching you to bend or ignore rules of grammar—not even slightly. That would be most inappropriate. There has never been a rule against beginning sentences with *'And'* or *'But.'* Witness this sample from the *Oxford English Dictionary.* It is acknowledged by scholars worldwide as the most respected authority on English usage:

GENERAL EXPLANATIONS.
THE VOCABULARY.

THE Vocabulary of a widely-diffused and highly-cultivated living language is not a fixed quantity circumscribed by definite limits. That vast aggregate of words and phrases which constitutes the Vocabulary of English-speaking men presents, to the mind that endeavours to grasp it as a definite whole, the aspect of one of those nebulous masses familiar to the astronomer, in which a clear and unmistakable nucleus shades off on all sides, through zones of decreasing brightness, to a dim marginal film that seems to end nowhere, but to lose itself imperceptibly in the surrounding darkness. In its constitution it may be compared to one of those natural groups of the zoologist or botanist, wherein typical species forming the characteristic nucleus of the order, are linked on every side to other species, in which the typical character is less and less distinctly apparent, till it fades away in an outer fringe of aberrant forms, which merge imperceptibly in various surrounding orders, and whose own position is ambiguous and uncertain. For the convenience of classification, the naturalist may draw the line, which bounds a class or order, outside or inside of a particular form; but Nature has drawn it nowhere. So the English Vocabulary contains a nucleus or central mass of many thousand words whose 'Anglicity' is unquestioned; some of them only literary, some of them only colloquial, the great majority at once literary and colloquial,—they are the *Common Words* of the language. But they are linked on every side with other words which are less and less entitled to this appellation, and which pertain ever more and more distinctly to the domain of local dialect, of the slang and cant of 'sets' and classes, of the peculiar technicalities of trades and processes, of the scientific terminology common to all civilized nations, of the actual languages of other lands and peoples. And there is absolutely no defining line in any direction: the circle of the English language has a well-defined centre but no discernible circumference*. Yet practical utility has some bounds, and a Dictionary has definite limits: The lexicographer must, like the naturalist, 'draw the line somewhere', in each diverging direction. He

—Oxford University Press

The odd thing about this taboo is that all of us read sentences every day beginning with '*And*' and '*But.*' But you have probably never noticed them. And that, incidentally, should be a clue to you that if you do it intelligently your readers will not notice it either.

As a matter of fact, if you are going to shorten sentences as we urged in Session 1, you will find that the connectives are an important part of the writing. They are bridges between ideas. True, as the English teacher says, they add nothing to the grammar. But they do add important flow. There is a logical meaning imparted by that word '*And.*' Still a different logical meaning imparted by '*But.*' Other connectives are equally important. Look for opportunities to begin sentences with words like '*Therefore,*' '*Next,*' '*Still,*' and many others. Do not deprive yourself of these important bridges of thoughts.

Here is an example of the importance of the connective. Notice the purpose the '*And*' and '*But*' serve:

Writing financial statements is very much like writing engineering or scientific reports. In each, those words on paper are the finished product of a great amount of work by a specialist. The concepts are difficult. Much of the vocabulary is specialized. And the people who must understand it may range from experts in the field to lay men and women.

These are difficult conditions at best. But the language principles that make writing clear are the same for all professions. And the poor accountants, engineers, and scientists—lawyers too, for that matter—must meet the challenge if they are to advance in their professions. Those who can present conclusions that are brilliant, clear, and concise are the ones whose work will be noticed and who will be chosen for promotions.

Unfortunately, colleges fail to impress this upon the young professional. . . .

Notice that same passage without the *'And'* or *'But'*:

Writing financial statements is very much like writing engineering or scientific reports. In each, those words on paper are the finished product of a great amount of work by a specialist. The concepts are difficult. Much of the vocabulary is specialized. The people who must understand it may range from experts in the field to lay men and women.

These are difficult conditions at best. The language principles that make writing clear are the same for all professions. The poor accountants, engineers, and scientists—lawyers too, for that matter—must meet the challenge if they are to advance in their professions. Those who can present conclusions that are brilliant, clear, and concise are the ones whose work will be noticed and who will be chosen for promotions.

Unfortunately, colleges fail to impress this upon the young professional. . . .

TABOO NO. 2 is at the ends of sentences: *THAT YOU MAY NOT END SENTENCES WITH PREPOSITIONS.* Of course you may. The alternative may be an awkward, unnatural sentence. We admit that prepositions are weak words. Therefore, when a sentence ends with one, it tends to dribble to a close rather than ending crisply. Still, that is sometimes a better choice than taking the long way around.

Perhaps the best known illustration of this point is a famous Winston Churchill story. Allegedly, Churchill was criticized for ending a sentence with a preposition, and he shot back: *"This is the type of arrant pedantry up with which I will not put."* There you have the awkward, unnatural sentence as an alternative to ending with a preposition.

TABOO NO. 3 is probably the most dangerous of all: *THAT YOU MAY NOT REPEAT WORDS.* You probably learned, "Use a word once. If you need it again, or at least if you need it very soon, you should find a synonym instead." That is terrible advice!

The issue here is *first-choice words.* When an intelligent adult uses a particular word—either intuitively or after careful thought to keep the writing clear—this is probably endorsement that it was the first-choice word for that situation.

The teacher tells you to seek other words for variety. But our objectives are *clarity and precision*—not variety. If your first-choice word was the correct one, but now you are forced to use something else, you go to a second-, third-, and fourth-choice word. Rather, re-use your first-choice word.

There are few exact synonyms in English; you usually go from specific to abstract when you seek them. But the abstract word may offer a choice of several specific meanings; therefore the writing becomes less precise.

Or you may mislead the reader by switching words. He or she may not realize you intended the two words to mean the same thing. For example, suppose you are writing about a warehouse. If you cannot use the word *'warehouse'* again, you might refer to it as the *'facility'* the second time. And the third time you might refer to it as the *'unit.'*

'*Unit,*' incidentally, is one of the misused words in the English language. Use '*unit*' only when you are referring to units of measure, such as 'unit price' or 'unit package.' But do not use '*unit*' as a universal synonym. Used that way, a unit is an industrial '*whatchamacallit.*'

By all means repeat first-choice words. Remember, the objectives when you are choosing words should be clarity and precision—not variety. *When you use second-, third-, or fourth-choice words, you are hurting your reader.*

To avoid too much repetition, the language gives us pronouns. You may refer to the warehouse as '*it*' or to two or more warehouses as '*they.*' Of course, you can do this only after establishing what 'it' or 'they' stands for by using the original word first. Putting it grammatically, pronouns need antecedents. Use pronouns as naturally in your writing as you would in conversation.

Let us repeat an important point about grammar, to prevent any possible misunderstanding. Although this course encourages you to throw off some old attitudes toward language, please do not get the impression that grammar is no longer important. Correct grammar is essential. It is just as important today as it ever has been. But grammar should not inhibit you. Most educated adults should have no trouble keeping their grammar correct unless they try to use sentences too long or complicated.

Good writing reads naturally. When it seems natural or desirable to begin a sentence with a connective, or end with a preposition, or repeat a good word, go ahead and do so. In these cases the writing will read so naturally the reader will not notice you did some things he or she may have been taught are wrong. *Remember, too, the three taboos are **not** rules of grammar and never have been.*

How Important Is Brevity?

From our discussion so far, you may have gotten the impression that good writing should be as brief as possible. Not so. In fact, that may be a risky attitude.

Although brevity is desirable, clarity is more important. Your reader measures the length of a report or letter by how long it takes to read. To the reader, therefore, brevity is more a function of clarity and good organization than of total length. (As we have already said, we will discuss organizing in the second half of this course.)

Fortunately, the same characteristics that make writing clear also make it brief. **Seek clarity, and the brevity will come. But if you seek brevity, two serious flaws may develop: First, you may leave out important information in your zeal to keep the writing short. Second, you may end up sounding blunt, and therefore unreasonable, by stripping the writing of those 'courtesy' words which create the image that you are a thoughtful and courteous human being.**

Certainly you should get rid of the padding—learn how to trim the fat without hurting the meat. But do not try to strip the writing down to the bare minimum of words. Prudent, intelligent people ought to be able to trim just enough but not too much—to keep their writing moving fast but not too fast.

By all means learn to recognize wasted words and knock them out of your writing. Some words add absolutely nothing but length. They are just there, contributing no meaning, no emphasis, no courtesy. They creep in because the author is too lazy to block them out. Sometimes they are worse than wasted; they may make the author look silly, as in the following passage:

you, if interested in making this acquisition, must do so on the basis that you will not, in all probability, enjoy the tax advantages which the present owners have been obtaining from the multiple corporate setup. Past experience shows that the Internal Revenue Service would take action to disallow the claiming of tax benefits resulting from the use of multiple corporations insofar as they are established primarily for that purpose. We were advised by Mr. Green that the multiple corporate setup had been started a number of years ago not to reduce taxes but in an effort to avoid being subject to the wage and hour law.

(34 words)

There you see some wasted words that make the author look silly. Like *'past experience.'* Is there any other kind? Likewise *'take action to,'* *'the claiming of,'* and *'insofar as'* add nothing. Without them, the passage says the same thing but in far fewer words:

you, if interested in making this acquisition, must do so on the basis that you will not, in all probability, enjoy the tax advantages which the present owners have been obtaining from the multiple corporate setup. Experience shows that the Internal Revenue Service would disallow tax benefits resulting from the use of multiple corporations established primarily for that purpose. We were advised by Mr. Green that the multiple corporate setup had been started a number of years ago not to reduce taxes but in an effort to avoid being subject to the wage and hour law.

(23 words)

But not all repetition is wasted. Wise authors sometimes repeat for emphasis. You may have noticed, for example, near the top of this page we said: "Some words add absolutely nothing but length." It is true that *'absolutely'* adds nothing to the meaning. But it does add emphasis. The statement is more forceful than if we had just said "Some words add nothing but length."

Another habit that adds unnecessary length to writing—and also makes it terribly heavy—is the habit of turning verbs into nouns. One of the surest ways to ruin writing is to ruin the verbs, turning them into other parts of speech. Verbs are action words. More than any other part of speech, therefore, they keep the ideas moving. But some writers, as though seeking to use extra words, turn desirable verbs into nouns, then rearrange the sentence so the verb becomes 'is' or something equally weak. Here is an example of that type of extra-long and extra-heavy writing. Notice how some key words are weakened:

Utilization of the computer in payroll preparation will bring about a reduction in clerical costs.

(15 words)

Here is that same passage again, shorter and clearer, the way most people would naturally say it:

Using the computer to prepare payrolls will reduce clerical costs.

(10 words)

We repeat: Brevity is desirable, but clarity is more important. Seek the clarity and the brevity will come. By all means get rid of wasted words, but do not sacrifice ideas to be brief. Also remember, stripping writing to the bone will usually cause the tone to sound blunt, overbearing. Courtesy is important. A pleasant, dignified image—perhaps even charm if you wish to call it that—should be a standard part of your writing. Your image is at stake.

• •

How alert were you? All of these important points were discussed in the videotaped presentation you just watched. You should be able to answer them all. If you cannot, look them up in this book.

When the writer uses passive voice verbs, he or she often fails to tell the reader:

by whom

What do all passives have in common that makes them easy to recognize?

form of the verb "to be"

Briefly describe the attitude Mr. Joseph recommends toward getting people into your writing:

Bring them into Writing - Refer to people and Companies by name.

What question should you ask yourself as an aid when having trouble expressing an idea clearly?

how would I say it in Conversation?

What warning should you keep in mind when using conversational style?

Be grammatically correct

For what important reason must writers sometimes begin sentences with connectives?

Smooth logical flow from sentence to sentence - Clarity & impact

What are the dangers of seeking synonyms rather than repeating words?

words rarely mean the same thing Confusion; lose of clarity

On keeping the writing brief, Mr. Joseph advises:

Seek ___Clarity___ and the ___brevity___ will come.

What two things may go wrong if you try to write in the fewest possible words?

curt, blunt writing
lack of clarity

SESSION 2
Exercises

EXERCISE 7.

Passive voice verbs rob your writing of precision by failing to tell *'by whom.'* The writer knows, but cannot see that he or she is withholding some valuable information from the reader.

Rewrite the following passage in the active voice. (But before you can, we must fill you in: The writer is reporting on, and giving his opinion of, a research project for his company by Purdue University.)

It is recommended that digital embedding be used, and it is believed that this can be done easily.

Your Rewrite

I recommend using digital embedding. It can easily be done

Course Recommends

EXERCISE 8.

Sometimes '*by whom*' is obvious or unimportant. Then the passive may be appropriate. Consider rewriting this passage in the active voice. But you may want to leave it passive:

After the storm, victims were aided by both police and volunteers. The rainfall is believed to be the heaviest of any 24-hour period in the city's history.

Your Rewrite

Police and volunteers aided the storm victims. The rainfall is believed to be the heaviest of any 24 hr period in the city's history

Course Recommends

EXERCISE 9.

Get people into your sentences. The writing will be more precise and sound more courteous. Do not introduce people artificially; simply do not go out of your way to block them out. Impersonal tone is no guarantee that you treated the subject objectively.

Try rewriting this passage in a more human way. Notice that making it warmer does not in any way affect the accuracy or dignity:

As of today's date, this office has succeeded in vacating 12 positions through retirement or reassignment. It is doubtful that an additional 20 positions can be similarly vacated before June 20.

It is hoped at all cost that the laying off of any employees can be avoided. Any assistance that can be rendered in this matter will be appreciated by the writer.

Your Rewrite

As of today's date, we have vacated
12 positions through retirement or
reassignment. I doubt that 20 additional
positions can be vacated before
June 20.
I will appreciate your assistance in
avoiding additional lay offs.

Course Recommends

EXERCISE 10.

Conversational style is a guide to the best way of writing most things. It will often make your writing clear and more gracious. The passage below is from a government memo, but principles of writing are the same regardless of the subject or the nature of the organization. Try writing this passage as you would **say it if you were face to face with your reader:**

Subsequent to removal of the sign from the right of way immediately upon notification of noncompliance, Ms. Andrews requested the Department to inform her of the procedures to follow in pursuing authorization to erect it legally. Although State and Federal regulations prohibit advertising on the right of way, I have directed Department staff to cooperate in helping Ms. Andrews identify areas wherein she can erect her sign in compliance with legal requirements.

Your Rewrite

Ms. Andrews asked the depart for information in posting ad sign used for advertising. She would like to re-erect it in an area that will comply with legal requirements. I have directed my staff to help her identify an area.

Course Recommends

_____
_____
_____
_____
_____
_____
_____

Caution: The listener will forgive a little carelessness. But the reader will not. You must be more careful in writing than in talking to keep the grammar entirely correct.

EXERCISE 11.

One of the surest and easiest ways to improve your writing is to avoid long, complex sentences. But shortening sentences may cause the ideas to sound choppy, unless you do something to restore the smooth, logical flow between the end of one idea and the beginning of the next. That is why connectives are so important—especially at the beginnings of sentences. There has never been any rule against beginning sentences with 'and' or 'but.'

Rewrite this passage, keeping both the clarity and impact of short sentences **and** the smooth logical flow of the connective:

Formerly, orders to customers in the East were handled through the Philadelphia warehouse. But now there is only a sales office in Pittsburgh serving all of Pennsylvania, and although four salesmen there generate approximately $2 million annually in sales, they do not make the final acceptance of any orders.

Your Rewrite

Course Recommends

EXERCISE 12.

Here is a grammar mistake in a government agency memo. The writer probably made it because he or she tried to break the ideas without a connective. Rewriting the passage should be easy:

While it is not possible to keep everyone advised on the changes by the Federal and State Commissions, and by the various other regulatory agencies as they occur. We will keep offices with specific problems advised. *And by the various*

Your Rewrite

_____

_____

_____

_____

_____

_____

_____

_____

_____

Course Recommends

_____

_____

_____

_____

_____

_____

_____

_____

_____

_____

EXERCISE 13.

Seeking synonyms, rather than repeating first-choice words, may cause imprecision. There are few exact synonyms; your second-choice word is usually more general. Even if you do find an exact synonym, using two different words to describe the same thing may mislead your reader; he or she may think you are referring to two different things.

The result will probably be confusion, as in this letter from a sales executive to a customer. The poor synonyms are underlined. Try to rewrite the letter without them. But be careful:

Dear Mr. Meisinger,

As you probably know, the 59th Annual Convention of the National Retail Merchants' Association was held in New York City January 7th through 11th. Our company gave a seminar at this meeting, on organization of retail stores and the use of computers.

Because you were unable to have a member present at this event, I thought you might like to review our presentation. We have reproduced it in the enclosed brochure, reprinted from the official proceedings of the exposition published by the Society.

We will be happy to provide you extra copies of this publication, if you would like them for other members of your management.

Your Rewrite

_____

_____

_____

_____

_____

_____

_____

_____

_____

_____

_____

_____

_____

_____

_____

(Continued on next page)

EXERCISE 13 Your rewrite (continued):

_____

_____

_____

_____

_____

_____

_____

**Course
Recommends**

_____

_____

_____

_____

_____

_____

_____

_____

_____

_____

_____

_____

_____

_____

_____

_____

EXERCISE 14.

Good writers are aware that clear expression usually ends up brief. But if you try deliberately to make the writing as short as possible, you may leave out ideas; or you may sound blunt, overbearing. Still, good writers learn to recognize and avoid wasted words—to trim the fat without hurting the meat. Try to recognize the wasted words and rewrite this passage without them.

While there is no time deadline placed on this project it seems that a period of approximately two months should be adequately long. It would appear to me that one possible approach to this task would be for someone from your office to visit with Mr. Gellert and find out exactly what his needs and requirements are and then submit an action plan listing in detail the steps necessary to accomplish fully the objectives set out in Mr. Sauer's letter.

• •

**Your
Rewrite**

_____

_____

_____

_____

_____

_____

_____

• •

**Course
Recommends**

_____

_____

_____

_____

_____

_____

_____

EXERCISE 15. (optional)

Content, not tone, makes writing official, or professional, or dignified. The tone of your letters and reports should at all times be pleasant yet courteous. Usually, the Six Principles of Clear Writing will create that tone. In fact, the quest to sound *official* or *professional* often makes writing dull, and much too long.

Government letters and reports are often that way. We describe their style as *bureaucratic* or *gobbledygook.* Here is such a letter. But as you try to rewrite it, remember that professional men and women, scholars, engineers, and scientists write their share of gobbledygook too, just as bad as this:

Monthly checks issued through this agency bear a duly authorized payment date of the 3rd of the month inasmuch as we are assigned that date under a staggered check issuance arrangement in affect among the various Federal agencies which issue monthly checks. The purpose, of course, is to avoid some of the cyclic difficulties that post offices, the Treasury Department, and other institutions would encounter if all Federal checks were mailed or made payable simultaneously each month.

Delivery of checks in advance of their payment dates creates further problems. On those occasions when checks were inadvertently released by a post office prior to the scheduled payment date, banks and other business institutions experienced certain difficulties, brought about when payees presented the instruments, marked payable as of the 3rd of the month, on the 2nd or earlier, in effect placing the business institution in the position of either honoring an illegal instrument or declining to do so and thereby antagonizing the payee.

This office is pleased to report, however, that appropriate arrangements have been made with the Post Office and Treasury Department to have checks issued through this agency delivered henceforth on the 2nd of the month whenever the 3rd is a Sunday or holiday. This should, it would seem, accomplish the result you had in mind.

Rewriting that letter will demand that you call on your imagination to fill in much missing information. Would any readers take that trouble? (Incidentally, did you notice a misused word?)

● ●

Your Rewrite

_____

_____

_____

_____

_____

_____

_____

_____

(Continued on next page)

EXERCISE 15 Your rewrite (continued):

_____

_____

_____

_____

_____

_____

_____

- -

**Course
Recommends**

_____

_____

_____

_____

_____

_____

_____

_____

_____

_____

_____

_____

EXERCISE 16.

SO FAR, THIS TRAINING PROGRAM has consisted of two kinds of activities. You have received advice on writing techniques, and you have performed (and discussed) exercises applying those techniques *to other people's writing.* Now you should be ready to apply the principles of clear writing *to your own writing.*

YOUR FIRST HOMEWORK ASSIGNMENT: Rewrite something you wrote on the job before this course began, applying everything that has been discussed so far. In this way, you will get important practice applying the principles of clarity to the kinds of writing you do on your job—without the burden of having to compose something new.

This *before and after* comparison may shock you. It should convince you of two important points: That you can do the things we have been talking about, and that you will like your writing the new way.

How long should it take? For most people, this assignment should require about one hour of your time.

How large should the sample be? About one page. It can be a complete letter or report, or part of a larger one.

How should you prepare it? Please turn in both versions. For the original, an actual file copy (or a reproduction of it) will do. Your rewrite should be typewritten, double spaced, with wide margins.

What if you have not written anything on the job? Something from an earlier job will do, or a sample of someone else's writing in your office, or perhaps a page from a term paper or other college report.

DO NOT OVERSIMPLIFY. Remember, writing consists of *what* you write and *how* you write it, and they are separate. You must not sacrifice *content* to achieve *clarity.* That would be a poor trade, and it is never necessary. Your rewrite should cover the subject in the same depth, and be just as accurate, as the original—in every detail—but in clearer language.

"Thanks to words,
we have been able
to rise above
the brutes. . . ."

—Aldous Huxley

Measuring Your Clarity

Since the beginning of this course, we have been discussing clarity—your ability to express your valuable ideas so clearly your reader cannot misunderstand them. Certainly, clarity is not new to you. What may be new to many people is that *difficult* subjects can be expressed clearly. Most people associate clear writing with *simple* subjects. As the subject gets harder, they assume so must the writing style. You have seen it that way most of your life.

But if you examine the reader's needs you find the opposite should be true. Difficult subjects need greater clarity. That means, again you must reverse an old, common notion. We have asked you to do that several times in this course. We repeat because it is so important: **The harder the ideas, the easier the words and sentences should be—if they are to be received accurately.**

The reason for this becomes evident when you consider that reading requires energy.

Physiologically, the reading process consists of two major steps. Here is what goes on in the brain as a reader reads: **First, the brain receives words and sentences—black marks on a page—and converts these into meaningful concepts. And second, it intelligently examines those concepts.** Again, that vital separation we have been mentioning since this course began—the total separation between *what* you write and *how* you write it, or the *ideas* the reader receives and the *words and sentences* through which he or she receives them.

At any given time, a reader has a given amount of energy to devote to the reading. And it must be divided those two ways. First, words and sentences; they will get as much energy as they demand. Whatever energy is left is available for the ideas.

What does this mean to you as a writer? Put yourself in the reader's position. Suppose someone were to write you a very simple idea, such as: *It's a nice day today*—but in words and sentences so heavy they demand 95 percent of your available energy. If that IDEA is so simple it demands only five percent of your available energy (or less) to understand, you can afford to spend that 95 percent for words and sentences. Communication will succeed. But trouble is in store if the writer uses words and sentences demanding 95 percent of the reader's energy to convey ideas that demand as much as six percent. In this case, communication cannot succeed. There is not enough energy, and part of the message will not be received.

This division of energy becomes especially critical if the writer tries to present difficult ideas—for example, the meaning of Einstein's Theory of Relativity. Now if communication is to succeed, the writer *must* keep the language simple, because now the reader will need most of that available energy for the IDEAS. Otherwise, there may not be enough for both, and then the reader cannot understand the ideas even though he or she might want to.

The more energy your reader uses on words and sentences, the less is available for the ideas. But the reader cannot decide how he or she will divide that energy. The writer decides this for the reader, because it is the writer who chooses those words and sentences.

Thoughtful writers are aware of this. Therefore, thoughtful writers are constantly asking themselves, "How can I tell? How can I measure whether my word/sentence workload is proper for the ideas?" It is for this phase of your writing that educators have given us readability formulas.

How hard is this passage to read?

share. The Indenture requires the redemption at par of $890,000 principal amount of debentures (less credits for converted debentures) each year beginning in 1995, authorizes the optimal redemption at par of an additional $890,000 principal amount of debentures in each year (non-cumulative) beginning in 1990 and further optional redemptions at any time at prices ranging from $105.375 to $100.25, until 1989 and at par thereafter.

> Loan agreements requiring the Company and its subsidiaries to maintain a consolidated net working capital, as defined in the credit agreement of September 16, 1984 of not less than $8,000,000 and limiting dividends, except in capital stock of the Company, and stock payments subsequent to December 31, 1983 to the consolidated net income accumulated after that date plus $500,000 (approximately $2,061,000 unrestricted at December 31, 1985) necessitated long-term borrowing in the amount of $3,750,000 to correct the deficiency of approximately $350,000 in working capital as of December 31, 1985.

The loan agreements also provide for restrictions on the declaration of dividends, stock payments and certain capital expenditures if net working capital, as defined in the credit agreement of September 16, 1984, is or would be less than $10,000,000.

Note D—Shares of Common Stock increased by 24,302 shares in 1985 through the issuance of a 3% stock dividend. Earned Surplus was charged in the amount of $559,858, representing $549.833 fair market value of stock issued and $10,025 paid in cash in lieu of fractional shares, and capital stock and capital surplus was credited for $121,000 and $4?? ... of fraction. There were no ch...

How easy is this one?

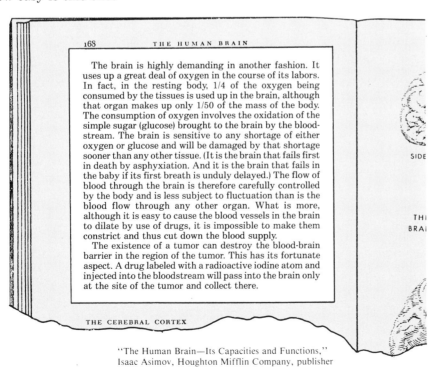

"The Human Brain—Its Capacities and Functions,"
Isaac Asimov, Houghton Mifflin Company, publisher

The Gunning Fog Index

Linguists have developed many formulas for measuring how easy or hard a piece of writing is to read, and these have been used and respected by educators since the early part of this century. They are based on sound education theory. Probably the best known of all the readability formulas is the Gunning Fog Index. Its author, Robert Gunning, was a leader in the crusade for clear writing until his death in 1980, and highly respected in education.

Gunning said difficult language fogs up the ideas, and this is a measure of how much fog. The formula is easy to use, and accurate. Here is how you figure readability using it:

Select the sample passage you wish to analyze. It may be any size, but no less than 100 words. And it must begin and end at a period. There are just three simple steps to this formula:

- **Step One. Figure the average number of words per sentence in the sample passage.** If it is your own writing, we hope you end up with a number between 15 and 20. Remember, you should be averaging between 15 and 20 words per sentence. (Principle Two of the Six Principles of Clear Writing.)

- **Step Two. Figure the percentage of hard words, or 'polysyllables,' in the passage.** Count as a polysyllable any word of three or more syllables. (With these three exceptions: First, proper nouns—that is, the capitalized names of people, places, companies, and products; count them as easy no matter how large they are. Second, combination words—large words made up of whole smaller words, such as 'horsepower,' or 'nevertheless,' or 'another' [which is literally 'an other']. Third, verbs that became three syllables by the addition of -ed, -es, or -ing such as 'inspected,' or 'receiving.')

In Step One you have measured the workload of your sentences by computing the average number of words per sentence in your sample, and you end up with a number. In Step Two you measured the workload of the vocabulary by computing the percentage of hard words, or polysyllables, and again you end up with a number. Then:

- **Step Three. Add the results of Steps One and Two, and multiply by .4. The final number is the Fog Index of that passage.**

Example: If a passage has 148 words and contains 8 sentences, that is an average of 18.5 words per sentence (148 ÷ 8). Note, incidentally, that without further figuring you have already learned that this author tends to divide ideas into sentences the proper length. If 16 of those 148 words are polysyllables, that is 10.8 percent (16 ÷ 148--divide the large number into the small one). Then 18.5 + 10.8 = 29.3; multiply by .4 (29.3 × .4 = 11.7). The Fog Index is 11.7.

WHAT SHOULD IT BE? For readable writing, the ideal Index is between 10 and 12. Anything between 8 and 14 is acceptable. Over 14, the writing is unnecessarily heavy. And over 17, it is unreadable for sustained reading. Anything under 8 might be perfectly accurate and clear, yet might offend by seeming childish.

You may be wondering, "What's the purpose of the .4?" Why not just add the results of Steps One and Two, then stop? The .4 converts the answer to years of education. *The Fog Index of a piece of writing corresponds to the number of years of formal education a reader of average intelligence would need, to read and understand writing at that word/sentence workload.*

Do not let this confuse or upset you. When we say your Readability Index should be between 10 and 12, we are not suggesting you should write 10th to 12th grade ideas. That would be unthinkable. Remember, writing consists of

FOG INDEX

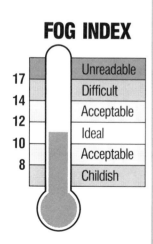

17	Unreadable
	Difficult
14	
	Acceptable
12	
	Ideal
10	
	Acceptable
8	
	Childish

what you write and *how* you write it. By all means, continue writing the highly adult, highly intelligent ideas you have been writing—but in words and sentences that demand no higher than 10th to 12th grade reading skills.

Remember too, the more difficult your ideas the more your reader should use energy on *them,* not on your words and sentences.

Analyzing your strengths and weaknesses. The Fog Index is a most useful tool. Use it to measure how clearly you have written. **But you can use it also to analyze *while* you are writing, to learn some valuable things about your writing habits. What are your strengths and weaknesses? What must you do to get rid of the weaknesses?**

Remember, any combination of Steps One and Two totalling between 25 (F.I. 10) and 30 (F.I. 12) is at a proper workload level.

Suppose, for example, in analyzing a passage you count 15 words per sentence and 15 percent polysyllables. Or 22 words per sentence and 8 percent polysyllables. Both total 30, for an Index of 12.

You can give the reader any combination totalling 30—even 25 words per sentence and 5 percent polysyllables; or 5 words per sentence and 25 percent polysyllables. At 25 words per sentence and 5 percent polysyllables, in effect readers are receiving easy information in large doses. At 5 words per sentence and 25 percent polysyllables, the information is very heavy but in mercifully small doses.

Linguists tell us that lay English usually requires about 10 percent polysyllables. For most business people, therefore, a combination of about 20 and 10 seems quite workable (20 words per sentence and 10 percent polysyllables). Engineers and scientists may need more polysyllables than that, if their subject demands a heavy vocabulary. For them we recommend 15 and 15. These are, however, just guides.

In some cases, you may not be able to control the vocabulary workload. But you can always control sentence length. If you need a heavy vocabulary, compensate by shortening sentences. Balancing the factors of the reader's workload this way will make a great difference in whether he or she understands your ideas.

BUT CAUTION: All readability formulas have one limitation. Regardless what formula you use, there is much about writing you cannot measure in numbers.

The Fog Index does give a statistically reliable measure of how difficult the sentences are. But it cannot measure whether the ideas progress logically from sentence to sentence. It does measure, quite reliably according to linguists and educators, how hard the words are. But no formula can measure if they were the right words in the first place.

Perhaps it is useful to compare a readability formula to a fever thermometer—a useful tool for measuring some important characteristics. The thermometer measures only *some* characteristics, not all. Still, no doctor would be without one. Too high or too low a temperature tells us something is wrong, but a proper temperature certainly does not ensure good health. Likewise, too high or too low a readability index tells us something is wrong, but a proper index does not ensure good writing. No originator of a readability formula ever claimed otherwise. (This paragraph has a readability index of 12.)

Therefore, let us say this about readability formulas: **A proper score is no guarantee of good writing. But a high score is a guarantee of bad writing.** If you accept that limitation, a readability formula may be useful in telling you some important things about your writing.

Remember too, these formulas measure *HOW* you write, not *WHAT* you write.

Pratt's Law

In large organizations such as government agencies, several people may have to approve everything you write. This can cause trouble, because they may not agree on what is or is not good writing. In fact, they may contradict each other.

Disagreement is especially common over how much detail a writer should include. The poor public servant may try to please the boss by including as much supporting information as possible in a report. That boss may be pleased, but the next one up the line says, "Too much detail. Burdens the reader. The chief will never approve this." The poor PS, then, removes the details, and the next boss up says, "Conclusions are unsupported by details."

At the Central Intelligence Agency, writers developed Pratt's Law as a guideline: "Whether you should include a large or small amount of details depends on whether there will be an even or odd number of reviewers."

(Also see: *Reviewing and Editing the Writing of Others,* page 111.)

The following report illustrates that total separation. It has a Fog Index of 24.1—totally unreadable. After it is a simpler version of the same ideas with a Fog Index of 11.6. Here is the difficult (original) version:

An experimental performance evaluation of a 6.02-inch tip diameter radial-inflow turbine utilizing argon as the working fluid was made over a range of inlet total pressure from 1.2 to 9.4 pounds per square inch absolute with corresponding Reynolds numbers from 20,000 to 225,000. (Reynolds number, as applied herein, is definable as the ratio of the weight flow to the product of viscosity and rotor tip radius, where the viscosity is determined at the turbine entrance condition.) Efficiency and equivalent weight flow increased with increasing inlet pressure and Reynolds number. At design equivalent speed and pressure ratio, total efficiency increased from 0.85 to 0.90 and static efficency from 0.80 to 0.84 with increasing Reynolds number, while the corresponding increase in equivalent weight flow was approximately 2 percent. The relationship established between experimentally determined efficiency and corresponding Reynolds number indicated that approximately 70 percent of turbine losses are associated with wall and blade boundary layers.

An investigation was made at design Reynolds number for determining the probable error of a single observation for measured variables and calculated quantities, with results from a 16 data point set indicating that the probable errors in total and static efficiencies were ± 0.009 and ± 0.008, respectively and that probable error is inversely proportional to Reynolds number.

The version with F.I. 11.6 (below) is thoroughly understandable, dignified, courteous, and short. And there has been absolutely no sacrifice of content:

A radial-flow turbine with a 6.02-inch tip diameter was tested at inlet total pressures from 1.2 to 9.4 pounds per square inch absolute. Corresponding Reynolds numbers ranged from 20,000 to 225,000. The working fluid was argon. (Reynolds number = weight flow ÷ product viscosity and rotor tip radius, with viscosity measured at turbine entrance conditions.)

Efficiency and equivalent weight flow increased as inlet-pressure and Reynolds number increased. At design equivalent speed and pressure ratio, total efficiency increased from 0.85 to 0.90 with increasing Reynolds number. Static efficiency increased from 0.80 to 0.84. Equivalent weight flow increased about 2 percent. There was some relationship between efficiency and Reynolds number. It showed that about 70 percent of turbine losses are wall and blade boundary layer losses.

Probable error in total efficiency, at design Reynolds number, was calculated to be ± 0.009, using a 16 data point set. In static efficiency this was ± 0.008. Probable error increases proportionately as Reynolds number decreases.

It is impossible to justify writing in the hard-to-understand style of the first version (previous page), when the author can make it as easy to understand as the rewritten passage—and with so little effort! How many textbooks have we all read (or tried to read) in a style similar to the first version of that report? Were the **ideas** hard to understand, or was the writing?

On Official Tone

Business men and women often feel they must write in a complicated style because they are expected to sound *'official.'* "After all," they reason, "it's official business so it should sound like it." Should it? Perhaps. But does *tone* make writing official, or does *content?*

Certainly your writing is official whenever its content is the business you are authorized by your employer to conduct on its behalf. But many people try to sound authoritative through writing style alone. They try to sound cold and impersonal. And in the process their writing ends up unclear, sometimes even menacing in tone.

Clarity, courtesy, and official content are the ideal combination for letters and reports of all kinds. Your writing is fully official, fully authoritative, whenever its *content* is proper—even if it sounds clear and courteous.

Here is a sample of writing typical of that artificial image of authority writers sometimes try to achieve through tone. You have surely seen writing like this:

the policy of the government to aid in the expansion of small businesses.

The duly executed forms should be submitted to the undersigned upon completion.

Yours truly,

B. L. Cruicci
Applications Officer

Here is the same thing again, this time in clear, courteous language. If the first version was official, this one must be too, because they both say the same thing:

the government's policy to help small businesses expand.

Please return the signed forms to me when you have completed them.

Yours truly,

B. L. Cruicci
Applications Officer

On Legal Writing

Another common habit that makes writing harder to understand than necessary is the use of legal tone, even when it is not needed. Misguided writers often try to make their writing sound better or more important than it really is by giving it some special impressive tone. We repeat this advice from Session 1 of this course: Impress with your *ideas,* not the sound of the *words* with which you express them.

Legal vocabulary is easy to imitate. In defense of the lawyers, much of it has special meaning in legal documents. But it is just not necessary in other kinds of writing—even for lawyers.

Vocabulary, however, is not the major problem with most legal writing. By far the greater trouble is sentence structure. There is a popular belief throughout the legal profession that periods create loopholes—that a qualifying statement must be in the same sentence as the idea it qualifies. Therefore, to avoid loopholes lawyers are trained to avoid periods. That advice is nonsense. In fact, it is dangerous. It can cause unbelievably long sentences—often a whole paragraph in length. They may be legally and grammatically correct, but they are sometimes impossible to understand and often cause court battles to determine their real meaning. They fail to communicate. In fact they hinder communication, as in this example:

Pursuant to the provisions of the Act, the employer is duly responsible for notification of subsequent revisions in the location of said employer's place of business, subject to termination of exemption in the event of failure to provide such notification.

The law requires that your company notify us if it changes its address. If it doesn't notify us, you may lose your exemption.

Even lawyers can write clearly, and should. Judges beg them to. More important, if **you** are **not** a lawyer you cannot in any way justify imitating legal style—unless you are trying deliberately to bluff your reader.

The writer who tries this legal style usually finds it is easy to achieve, on any subject. But it will not impress. It will only succeed in making your writing harder than necessary to read and understand.

On Scientific Writing

The same things we said about legal writing (previous page) are also true of scientific tone. Some writers try to make ideas sound better than they are by expressing them in complex scientific language—even when it is not necessary. People in the so-called "human sciences"—educators, psychologists, and sociologists—seem notorious for this, but they are by no means the only ones. Here is an example:

Milwaukee: The National Learning Conference, 1984), pp. 207-211.

Integration of aural and visual stimulae produces a more intensified effect in the brain than those resulting from either modality's acting as a single class or type of stimulus.

It is suspected that the same or similar rationale lies behind both the practical and theoretical application . . . .

Here is what that really means:

Milwaukee: The National Learning Conference, 1984), pp. 207-211.

People learn better by hearing and seeing the ideas than by either one alone.

We suspect that the same or similar rationale lies behind both the practical and theoretical application . . . .

Notice, incidentally, that in the original passage the writer tried to use words more difficult than necessary and lost control; '*stimulae*' should be '*stimuli.*'

All of which prompts us to conclude: **Scientific vocabulary is a shabby substitute for scientific objectivity.**

• •

How alert were you? All of these important points were discussed in the videotaped presentation you just watched. You should be able to answer them all. If you cannot, look them up in this book.

Describe briefly how the reader must divide his or her energy while reading.

Sentence / words   1. Receiving words idea / converting into idea

idea   2. Examine idea

How does the writer influence the reader's ability to understand?

By the words and sentences written – determines how much energy will be spent where

Please complete this important sentence: The more ~~complex~~ *different* *the ideas,*

the ~~~~ *easier* *should be the* ~~old or them~~ *(words & sentences).*

List the three steps in figuring the Fog Index.

1. Figure average number words/sentence

2. Figure percentage hard words (polysyllables)

3. Add 1 + 2 & X .4

What should be the Fog Index range for ideal writing? 10 – 12

What is the highest acceptable Fog Index? 14 *The lowest?* 8

What is the danger if the Fog Index is too low?

Childish

In addition to measuring readability, how can the Fog Index help you analytically to improve your writing?

points out strengths & weaknesses

What warning must you keep in mind when using **any** *readability formula?*

Can tell you what's wrong but not what's right

Scientific Vocabulary *is a shabby substitute for*

scientific Objectivity.

SESSION 3
Exercises

EXERCISE 17.

Figure the Fog Index of these two passages:

However, it is now our considered opinion that in the light of recurring labor problems in the Brooklyn area, in contrast with a very satisfactory posture of labor in the Staten Island section of the port, and with the presence of the Verazanno Bridge—which has largely eliminated the time element which theretofore was enjoyed by piers in the Brooklyn area—we should make a decision to henceforth discharge all inward cargoes at Piers 19 and 20, Staten Island, until such time as it is demonstrated that the service in Staten Island to our clients is not at least the equivalent of that which has been provided in the Brooklyn area.

words per sentence:

+ percent polysyllables:

_Gunning FoG
measures sustained
reading._

_____

x .4

_____

Fog Index:

• •

Tungsten can be sintered to high densities at low temperatures if it is alloyed with elements such as nickel. However, an insoluble grain boundary phase makes such alloys weak at high temperatures. This work shows that these alloys are strong if certain third elements, such as copper, are added. The third element makes the nickel soluble in tungsten during sintering. The result is a dense, single-phase alloy that is strong at high temperatures. It can be rolled using standard techniques. The technique of producing precision parts of such alloys was developed by metallurgists at the National Aeronautics and Space Administration.

words per sentence:

+ percent polysyllables:

_____

x .4

_____

Fog Index:

• •

Before You Begin Part Two . . .

If you have learned all the things discussed in Part One—and can apply them to your writing—your reports, letters, and memos are probably very clear by now. But do not worry if you are having a bit of trouble applying these techniques. Not yet, anyhow. You may need practice to break old habits. As long as you must stop and think, and deliberately force yourself to apply the Six Principles of Clear Writing, you may be writing more slowly than before. There is nothing difficult about these principles, however, except breaking habits. Once you can apply the Six Principles naturally to your writing, without deliberately forcing yourself, you should gain the speed we have promised you.

But remember, clarity should not require any sacrifice of the intelligence, or detail, of the CONTENT of your writing. Again, writing consists of two things: *what* you write and *how* you write it, or your *ideas* and the *words and sentences* with which you convey them. When we say your writing should be as simple as possible, we are referring to the how, not the what. By all means, continue writing highly adult, highly dignified ideas—but in words and sentences that demand as little reader energy as possible, so your reader can devote most of his or her energy to the ideas.

Part Two
On Organizing

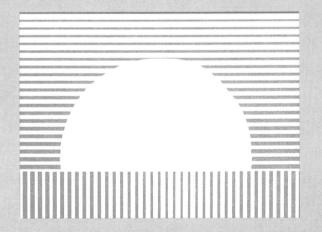

"Words are like leaves; and where they most abound, much fruit of sense beneath is rarely found."

—Alexander Pope

SESSION 4

Practical Tips on Organizing

The principles of clarity discussed in Part One apply to all kinds of writing—whether a business or engineering report, a newspaper article, or the great American novel. The advice in Part Two, however, applies only to that kind of writing we call 'expository.'

All writing is divided into two categories: expository or narrative. It is expository if its purpose is purely to convey information—either to inform or to persuade. All business writing, and most newspaper writing, is expository. Add one more ingredient, plot, and the writing becomes 'narrative.' Now the reader is reading not only for the information, but also for the interesting order in which the writer presents it. We repeat: The principles of organization presented here are only for expository writing. In fact, these principles would hinder your ability to develop a plot.

We can sum up all there is to say about organizing expository writing with this one statement: **Start with your conclusion, then spend the rest of the writing supporting it.** Everything you do is for the busy reader's needs, as with the principles of clarity.

You can learn valuable lessons about organizing expository writing by examining a good newspaper article. Journalism experts have conducted detailed surveys to discover how readers read, and they have learned some things you should know about readers of expository information.

The expository reader is in a hurry to stop. This is not a criticism; the reader is not lazy. It is simply that the expository reader is reading only for information. He or she is busy and eager to stop reading as quickly as he or she has all the important information. That is especially true if your reader is a top executive.

Your job is to tell as much as possible, as clearly and accurately as possible, in as little reading as possible. That is true whether you are writing a business letter or memo, or a complicated engineering report. Never make readers wonder, '*What are you getting at?*' Get to the point as fast as possible. There are some exceptions, which we will discuss later. But generally it is unwise to build up gradually to your most important information at or near the end.

Putting your conclusions *at the beginning* satisfies all possible readers. **If your reader wants only the most important information, placing it first guarantees he or she will get the information *you* considered most important. Or, some people may be interested in reading every word in detail. Or perhaps your reader wishes to read selectively—some passages but not others. When you write, you cannot be sure how much detail readers may want. But by putting your conclusions first, then following with the supporting details, you give any reader the choice.**

Even if your reader intends to read every word in great detail, he or she is a better reader having received the conclusion first. Reading experts tell us an *OVERVIEW* is important if the reader is to understand—especially for difficult information. Without it, you give the receiving brain isolated bits of information; that is unwise. First declare what the brain is going to receive; then those bits of information are no longer isolated. **Armed with that overview, the reader will understand the details better and retain them longer.**

There is still another reason you should get to the point fast. If you do not tell the reader in advance what your important points are, he or she might arrive at some conclusion other than you intended. The results may be disastrous. Do not let that happen to your writing. *You* control what your reader gets out of your writing by declaring early what he or she *should* get out of it.

The Inverted Pyramid

To satisfy the reader's need for the overview near the beginning, journalists have created the Inverted Pyramid Structure. That term should be important to your writing the rest of your life. The Inverted Pyramid is the structure which presents the most important information early, then spends the rest of the writing supporting it.

Here is what it looks like in its simplest form:

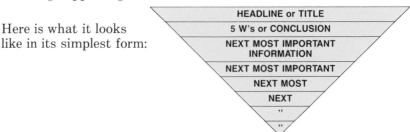

Notice that the simplest Inverted Pyramid is heavy at the top and fades into nothingness at the bottom. That is how most newspaper articles are organized. And it is how all reports and most letters should be organized. The realistic writer starts with the attitude that the reader may be interested in reading only a small part of the writing, especially if it is a report. Therefore, he or she puts everything the reader **must** learn into the early paragraphs.

The 5 W's of journalism. To ensure that the writer puts the most important information at the beginning, writers centuries ago created the "*5 W's*" of journalism: *Who, What, When, Where, and Why.* These go in the first paragraph. They ensure that the reader gets the most important information even if he or she reads no further. Who, What, When, Where, and Why—though not necessarily in that order.

Your letters and reports may not have all five of the W's. You may have just one—*What.* More likely, two—*What* and *Why.* Look for that vital information you most want your reader to receive—the one idea about which you would be willing to say: "*It's all right if my reader learns nothing else.*" That conclusion, or overview statement, is the real reason for the writing. Declare it at the beginning—especially in a report. Otherwise, the reader may learn little or nothing—or arrive at some conclusion other than you intended.

Why write the rest? You may ask, "*If the reader gets all the significant information in only a fraction of the writing, why go through all the trouble of writing pages and pages of support?*" In most cases, you write the rest to clarify to the reader how you arrived at the key points in the overview statement. Your reader may choose to read the entire report beginning to end, or just the overview statement. Any reader is entitled to that choice. But even if the choice is to read only the overview information, any reader is comforted by the presence of the supporting documentation. Take away that supporting documentation, and he or she may not trust what you have said in the overview.

Structuring the rest. Once you have written the overview, there are basically three ways you can organize the rest of the information that makes up the whole Inverted Pyramid: **in order of importance (usually most desirable for readers), in logical order, or in chronological order.** (There is a fourth way: chaos. And if it is not one of the first three, it will surely be number four.)

Here is an example of the beginning of a letter organized as an Inverted Pyramid. Notice it gets to the point fast:

Ms. Falberg,

As you requested, we have thoroughly examined the operations of XYZ Company's Blodgett Division. We found no serious weaknesses.

A few of your practices we feel are inefficient. We have listed these by department, along with detailed suggestions for improvement. All of these suggested changes can be made with your existing staff, but a few will require new equipment. In all cases, the savings brought about by the change will pay for the new equipment in less than a year. May I stress, however, that these are all minor suggestions...

Notice that the writer gives the summary or conclusion in the first paragraph. The reader learns immediately that the writer found no serious weaknesses. Then, quickly, the reader also learns that the Blodgett Division has a few inefficient practices, and that detailed explanations follow for each department. All of that information is the overview. The rest of the letter, although it is not shown here, gives the details. The simplest Inverted Pyramid would describe the departments one by one. Perhaps they would be listed in order of importance—or perhaps geographically, or by some other logical pattern. Each section, incidentally, might be structured as a minor Inverted Pyramid—with its own conclusion at the beginning. Many variations are possible for the details, but they all have one thing in common: They are unified by a strong opening statement.

How to end a report: There is no need for a summary or wrap-up statement at the end. Writers like to end dramatically; readers do not care. In fact, a proper Inverted Pyramid encourages most readers to stop early, by making it easy to do so reliably. So most readers will never know—or care—how you ended. **The best advice on how to end seems to be: When you have nothing more to say, just stop.**

This is the opposite of the advice recommended for public speaking. If you have studied public speaking, you probably learned: *'Tell them what you are going to say; then say it; then tell them what you have said.'* That is an excellent guide for public speaking. But in writing, do not feel you must use a dramatic ending. Many of the best writers—newspaper columnists for example—usually do not use it. We repeat: When you have nothing more to say, just stop.

Inexperienced writers often resist the idea of the Inverted Pyramid. There are two common reasons:

First, putting the conclusion at the beginning is probably the opposite of your natural tendency. To do so requires that you reverse the order of your thinking. Writers tend to tell things in the order in which they learned them. When you do, you are writing a diary, or time sheets. There is usually no relationship between the order in which you learned your information and the order in which your reader should learn it. If your thinking is open-minded, you usually gather the supporting information first, then examine it, and arrive at the conclusions and recommendations last. But that is usually the worst possible order for the reader.

Second, writers often resist the Inverted Pyramid because their pride is hurt by the idea that the reader may not read every word. This is especially true if you have done a good job and know it, and the reader is your boss. You want every reader to study every word from beginning to end; you want your good work to be recognized. But it is unreasonable to expect a reader to read for the purpose of noticing what a good job the writer did.

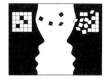

A Recommended Format for Formal Reports

For most reports and letters, a simple Inverted Pyramid structure is usually easy to construct. But the longer a piece is, the harder it is to organize. And, of course, it is the long ones that most need to be well organized.

There is no one format that works best for all reports. But you may find the following format useful as a guide, tailoring it to fit your particular body of information.

There are eight basic sections to this recommended structure. You may not need them all. In fact, using them all would set up a very, very formal report such as an engineering or scientific research report. Here are the eight sections, in the order in which the reader reads them. *But note that you cannot possibly write them in that order;* **in fact, you must write them in the exact opposite order.** You will understand why as you see what they contain:

- **Title.** A good title can be immensely useful. Write it carefully. It should be a highly condensed version of the whole report. It should tell the subject and, if possible, the conclusion. (Most people omit the conclusion. Without it, you are not writing a title but a subject line.) Limit it to 120 typewritten characters or less—preferably much less.

- **Abstract.** This is a capsule version of the whole report. It tells subject, conclusions, and how you arrived at those conclusions. Limit it to 50 to 100 words. The abstract appears in library files, computerized information retrieval systems, and abstract journals; it does not appear in the report. If you need one, write it after the body and other preliminary sections. Otherwise it may not contain the right key words, and future literature search will be inaccurate as a result.

- **Summary.** This is the most important section of most reports. The summary contains exactly the same information as the abstract—subject, conclusions, and how you arrived at those conclusions—but in more detail. It is the first thing the reader reads after the title, and perhaps the only thing. Limit it to 200 to 300 words—to fit on one page.

- **Introduction.** Do not confuse this with the summary or abstract. The introduction should give background information—reasons for doing the work, possible benefits, past work on the subject, etc. Limit it to one page, or 200 to 300 words.

- **Conclusion.** Think hard here, to say what is really of significance. Do not be misled by the word 'conclusion.' This is not the conclusion of the report in the sense of 'concluding remarks.' Rather, it is the conclusion of the work you are reporting. And that is usually the last thing you learned while doing the work. Limit it to 50 to 100 words. If you need more, you probably have not thought enough: *What is the real meaning of this report?*

- **Recommendations.** This section is optional. Your conclusions may be your recommendations. Or you may have none. But if you do make recommendations, you are entitled to state your reasons for them briefly up front—especially if they may surprise or upset your reader. This is where you do it. Limit this section to one page, or 200 to 300 words.

- **Discussion.** This is the main body of the report. Describe your work and reasoning in all its detail. If you have done everything else correctly, the body can run hundreds of pages without inconveniencing the reader. But if it runs longer than a page or two, try to break it into sub-sections with separate sub-headings. (In that case, a table of contents might be useful up front.)

- **Appendixes.** Try not to use them. Put charts, tables, etc. in the body where you discuss them, unless there are too many. If possible, limit appendixes to optional information.

Notice there is some planned repetition in this format—particularly in the early sections. But each time, the reader gets more detail. If you put the proper information into these sections, you are forced to write an Inverted Pyramid. Your reader gets the choice of reading just a highly condensed version, or the condensed version followed by all the details, or the condensed version followed only by those details he or she chooses to read.

But notice too, as we said before, *you cannot possibly write these eight sections in the order you just read them.* That is the order in which your reader receives them. **You must write them in the OPPOSITE order.** Write the body first, planning it as an overall Inverted Pyramid. Then write the preliminary sections. Especially, you should write conclusion, summary, abstract, and title last. Each one is a progressively more condensed version of the body. Therefore, you cannot possibly write them intelligently until you have written the body. If you write them first, you are doing them before you have done the major thinking, and those preliminary sections may not accurately reflect the body. That is a common flaw. It is probably the reason so many reports are hard to retrieve from the files; they are indexed and filed under the wrong words because the title and abstract may not contain the right words. Why not? Because the author wrote them in advance. Nobody will ever know how much duplicated research this has caused.

Your report may not contain all of these sections. Or it may contain these plus others. Again, this format is only a guide. It is reasonable to presume, however, that any serious report will have at least a title, summary, and body.

Far more important than following a rigid format, you must understand the theory of the Inverted Pyramid and why it works. If you do, you can intelligently design a format for each report to fit the information that particular report contains.

The Inverted Pyramid's One Disadvantage

You should be aware there is one disadvantage to the Inverted Pyramid. Putting the conclusion at the beginning does not allow you to be very subtle. Sometimes this structure may be too hard-hitting for the presentation of bad news. If the conclusion is likely to upset your reader, telling it first might close his or her mind to the supporting facts. In that case, you might deliberately choose to *start with the supporting information*—slowly but inevitably leading up to the conclusions or recommendations in such a way that the reader cannot escape them.

Never do that in a report, however. You may put the conclusion at the end in a letter if you wish, because a letter is short and addressed to one person, and you can reasonably assume that person will read the whole thing. In reports, the conclusion should always appear **at the beginning**.

More important, do not put your conclusions at the end simply for that worn-out reason, *'We've always done it that way.'* In business writing, so often the old way is the worst possible way. And so often we find the reason it is done that way is simply that nobody ever took the trouble to question: *'Is there a better way?'*

A Checklist for Organizing

Structure is harder to measure than clarity. There is no formula like the Fog Index. No one has devised a way to measure numerically whether ideas are arranged in some orderly sequence. Yet some way of evaluating—some checklist—is helpful.

It is reasonable to expect a few things of any piece of expository writing if it is to be well structured. These four questions might make a helpful checklist, especially for reports:

- Is there a summary or overview statement very early?
- Is all the information in some helpful sequence?
- Is the emphasis of the various ideas in proportion to their importance?
- Are there headings to help the reader?

Is there a summary or overview statement very early? Remember, the reader has the right to read only that if he or she chooses. He or she should not have to read very long or work very hard to find it. Remember too, even the reader who intends to read every word can understand the details better having had the overview first.

Is all the information in some helpful sequence? Perhaps the sections are arranged by order of importance. Perhaps by chronological order, or by company division or by product. But some order is demanded from beginning to end, and it should be obvious even to a scanning reader.

Is the emphasis of the various ideas in proportion to their importance? Two factors suggest how important an idea is, even before it is read: its size and its location.

The larger the section, the more important it looks. However, often a writer goes into great detail about an idea—not because it is important but because he or she is particularly well-informed about it and therefore enjoys writing about it. Expand the ideas in proportion to their importance to the reader, not your likes and dislikes, or you risk misleading the reader.

Also, the closer up front an idea appears, the more important it looks—unless it is obvious that you are arranging by chronological order or by some other order that demands lesser information early.

Are there headings to help the reader? Headings and sub-headings are like road signs, guiding the reader on his or her trip. We will talk about them in detail in Session 6. For now, let us say no report can be considered well structured without them, especially if it is very long.

WE REPEAT: When structuring your letters or reports, your job is to tell as much as possible, as clearly and accurately as possible, in as little reading as possible. The reader should not have to work very hard to receive your ideas. That is the way you want it when you are the reader. Always the reader. **Everything you do in writing—in both clarity and organization—is for the benefit of that person at the receiving end. He or she is the only reason you write.**

What one statement sums up the advice on organizing expository writing?

Start with the conclusion, then spend the rest of the writing supporting it.

The Inverted Pyramid structure gives the reader two choices, both good. Please describe them.

1. *read entire report*

2) *read overview only.*

What are the three ways of arranging the body of a report, after the opening?

importance

logical order

Chronological

Which of these is usually the most desirable for the reader? *importance*

What is the best advice for ending a report? *just stop*

Why is the reader a better reader having had the overview first?

Knows what to look for — what you're trying to say

For what two reasons do writers often resist writing Inverted Pyramids?

Seems backwards

pride hurt in balance isn't read

Please list the eight sections of a formal report, in the order in which the reader reads them.

title, abstract, summary, introduction, conclusion recommendation Body, appendices

What is the difference between that order and the order in which the writer must write them?

Backwards

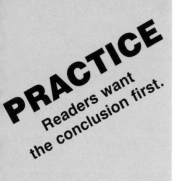

SESSION 4
Exercises

EXERCISE 18.

The Inverted Pyramid structure helps readers by giving the important information as quickly as possible, in as little reading as possible.

The hardest thing about writing an Inverted Pyramid is planning: What should be the opening statement? What one statement, or short group of statements, sums up the whole piece of writing?

The memo below is well written in its words and sentences, but it is poorly organized. The writer simply put things down in the order in which they happened. That is a common mistake, because it is easy. It is almost like a fairy tale beginning *'Once upon a time . . .'* and ending *'They all lived happily ever after.'*

Restructure the memo so it gives the reader the most important information first:

Bumstead Tool Company opened a credit card account with us on July 15, 1984. In October 1984 they began falling behind in payments.

After the usual collection letters, we put the company on our delinquent list and cancelled their credit. At that time they owed $2,372.09. I phoned Mr. H. D. Bumstead, company president, on April 2, and he promised to send us the full amount within 30 days. I also requested that the company return our three credit cards.

That was 30 days ago. We have received the credit cards but no money.

This customer shows no willingness to cooperate. The Retail Credit Bureau reports they are unable to pay other bills. I recommend that this account be turned over to our legal department for further action.

Mr. Bumstead was formerly sales manager of Western Tool Company. They have been a good customer of ours for many years. He formed Bumstead Tool Company July 1, 1984.

**Your
Rewrite**

_____

_____

_____

_____

_____

_____

_____

_____

(Continued on next page)

EXERCISE 18 Your rewrite (continued)

_____

_____

_____

_____

_____

_____

_____

**Course
Recommends**

_____

_____

_____

_____

_____

_____

_____

_____

_____

_____

_____

_____

EXERCISE 19.

This memo is structured as a narrative, starting with introductory information and leading in logical order to its most important statement *at the end*. One simple change corrects this. Make that change, rearranging the information into the Inverted Pyramid structure:

Most designers believe that stress figures obtained from photographs are more accurate than those computed electronically. This is probably because photointerpretation takes longer. However, in many cases electronic results are more accurate.

Analysts have the training necessary to determine which method will give the most accurate results for a particular job. They, not the designers, should decide whether photointerpretation or electronic data should be used. Please instruct all designers in your branch that they should not specify the method of measuring stress data on future jobs.

Your Rewrite

_____

_____

_____

_____

_____

_____

_____

Course Recommends

_____

_____

_____

_____

_____

_____

_____

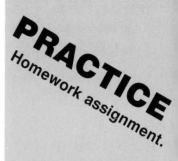

EXERCISE 20.

THIS IS THE BACKGROUND: Many companies in recent years have set up a department whose purpose is to analyze and evaluate other departments. This is usually called the Systems and Procedures Department, Operations Research, Management Services Audit, etc. Its staff members are usually experts at spotting troubles and recommending solutions.

In the Acme Widget Division, this Department is called the Systems and Procedures Branch (S&P). The manager reports directly to the vice president of operations. Acme is a leading manufacturer of heavy duty widgets and is known for high quality products and reliable service. The home office is in Ithaca, N.Y., with manufacturing plants there and in St. Louis. Sales and service offices exist in major cities throughout the United States and Canada.

As S&P increased in size and scope at Acme the past few years, other departments began to regard its activities with suspicion. Today, depending on whom you talk to, S&P is called everything from "A necessary evil" to "a bunch of half-ass college-bred snoopers." Almost every management-level employee has heard by word of mouth that the department raises havoc with work routines when it undertakes investigations; that its recommended methods are usually less efficient than the old way; and that even if the new way is more efficient, it does not save enough to justify the cost of operating the S&P department. "Our savings are paying their salaries" has been a frequent complaint.

When S&P employees go out into the field to study an operation, the instructions from the Home Office are that they should be given full cooperation. But regional managers often take the attitude that no news from the home office is good news—especially when S&P is concerned. Such managers do little to conceal that attitude from the employees beneath them. As a result, the S&P auditors encounter resistance more often than cooperation.

Recently, Gayle Timmons and Harold Giardino, two young auditors from the Systems and Procedures Department, were assigned to do a systems and cost analysis of the work involved in receiving and answering a typical service call in the Salt Lake City Regional Office. Why Salt Lake City? Because records at the Home Office showed that service costs were lower there than in any other Region. Salt Lake City must be doing something the other Regions could profit from learning.

The usual announcement went out to the Regional Manager announcing that the S&P auditors would be arriving, and making clear that the company expected them to be given full cooperation in anything they requested.

Monday morning Timmons and Giardino arrived, expecting to spend a full week. They wanted to talk to the manager, several sales representatives, the repair crews, and the order clerks.

They spent the first morning with the Regional Manager, touring the operation and being introduced to other key personnel. Everything was cordial. But at lunch, which was the first time they were alone with the manager, they sensed hostility. After 45 minutes of small talk, he admitted the entire staff was not too happy when they received the announcement that S&P was going to examine every operation; their presence, it was widely believed, implied that the Home Office doubted everyone's skills—from management down. The auditors tried to explain that the Home Office wanted to point up Salt Lake City as a **good example** for the other regions to follow—in that sense their presence should be a compliment. Still, the manager was skeptical and it showed. He assured them, however, that he had instructed everyone in the region to cooperate in anything required of them for the survey.

"Oh, by the way," the manager said as they were getting up from lunch, "don't be upset by the service department manager. He's been here sixteen years, and his repair crews are the best in the West. But he's touchy about criticism." The manager seemed edgy. The S&P auditors, comparing notes later, both sensed he was afraid they were going to louse things up.

Tuesday morning Timmons and Giardino were finally able to talk with the service manager. He talked politely about fishing in Utah and a few other trivial subjects. But when they tried to talk business he seemed unwilling to listen to their explanation of the purpose of their study, let alone cooperate with them. He could not prevent them from talking to the repair crews, but he made it clear he did not expect they would learn much. "We'll cooperate," he reassured them. "My people are good enough they can give you anything you want without slowing down a bit."

The repair personnel were obviously talented, well trained, and well managed. They too, however, did not believe the true purpose of the S&P visit. They seemed friendly, even joking with the visitors. Or were they joking **at** them? It soon became obvious they weren't going to tell much—at least not in language the Home Office dudes could understand. One of them even commented on the third day, when the visitors accompanied them on service calls, that they didn't have much respect for (1) young college kids, and (2) people who come around as experts in widget repair but can't repair one.

Although Timmons and Giardino were intimately familiar with all aspects of the design, manufacture, and marketing of heavy-duty widgets, it was true they could not repair one. So they spent three hours Wednesday night studying a repair manual—even memorizing the names of the parts. In this way they hoped to win the cooperation of the repairmen in the field. To win acceptance from the service department manager, they also decided to appeal to his interest in fishing; they bought outdoors magazines at the hotel newsstand and spent several more hours reading them.

Thursday and Friday the auditors were slightly more successful. But as they headed home Friday night and began planning their report, both agreed their S&P study had been seriously hampered by the attitude of the entire service group. As a result, their data was rather shallow, and they could probably not make recommendations that would benefit the other regions. The week's trip was probably not worth the effort. END OF BACKGROUND.

YOUR SECOND HOMEWORK ASSIGNMENT: You are one of those S&P auditors. The two of you have decided that you should be the one to write the report to management on this trip. That report is your assignment.

The heart of the lesson is this: To provide a proper overview, the opening paragraph should summarize *all* of the important points contained in the whole report— the information about which you would be willing to say, "It's all right if my reader reads nothing else." (This is an extension of the Inverted Pyramid theory. The writer's job is to convey as much information as possible, as clearly and accurately as possible, *in as little reading as possible.*)

Your full Salt Lake City report, therefore, would certainly contain, among other things, sections stating in detail that the project failed, why it failed, and what should be done about it. Those are surely the most important things your reader needs to know. They are, then, the things that should appear (briefly) in your overview statement, or summary. The rest of the report gives the supporting details, and includes any other information you consider less important.

DO NOT WRITE a full formal report with the eight sections discussed in Session 4; that would be too much for this situation. Your trip report can be in the form of a memo, or a short report with just a few sections.

Remember: This exercise is to evaluate the clarity and structure of your writing, not your ability to analyze the business problem and arrive at the best solution—**how** you write, not **what** you write.

PLEASE BE SURE your paper is typewritten, double spaced, with wide margins.

· ·

**Your
Rewrite**

_____

_____

_____

_____

_____

_____

_____

_____

_____

_____

_____

_____

_____

_____

_____

_____

_____

_____

"The outline, or plotline, is the architecture of writing; the words and sentences are the interior decoration."

—Ernest Hemingway

How to Outsmart the Deadline

If you understand the reader's needs and the advantages of the Inverted Pyramid structure, organizing properly should not be difficult—at least for your simple reports and letters. But structuring the ideas intelligently becomes much more difficult on your large writing jobs, such as major reports. And, of course, they are the ones that most need careful structuring.

Most people have trouble getting started on those major writing jobs. Ironically, conscientious writers usually have the greatest trouble. Careless people have no trouble at all getting started. But thoughtful writers do, because they want to start correctly. They recognize—consciously or subconsciously—something immensely important in writing: *The way you treat the beginning of a piece of writing will determine the character of the whole piece.* Or, as the old saying goes, "As the twig is bent, so grows the tree." That is certainly true in report writing. So, wisely, the careful writer tries to start correctly.

But that may be the most difficult part of writing. Typically, you sit down the first day of a major writing job with marvelous intentions. However, nothing happens; you sit staring at a blank page. After 15 or 20 minutes, you finally give up and say, "I'll write it tomorrow." When tomorrow comes, you are no better able to write. You put it off a second day, then a third and fourth.

Eventually, you do write that report. When? At the deadline.

You are not alone if you have been able to do your best writing only under the pressure of the deadline. Even great novelists have often reported this about themselves. Having trouble getting started is almost a universal phenomenon, and it is especially common among business men and women.

What is it about deadlines that helps us get started? What does the deadline force you to do differently?

The A-B-C Experiment

This simple experiment demonstrates why most people have trouble getting started writing, and why they actually **can** write better when the deadline arrives.

Ask a friend how many different combinations (permutations) can be made of the letters A and B, and to name them. There are two: AB and BA. Now ask that person how many combinations can be made of A, B, and C, and to name them—*without writing them*. There are six: ABC, ACB, BAC, BCA, CAB, and CBA. (An easy way to remember: Note there are three possible starting letters, and for each one there are two ways of arranging the second and third. Mathematicians call this pattern "three factorial.")

Most people cannot recite the six combinations of A, B, and C.

Next, ask how many combinations are possible with A, B, C, and D (four factorial), and ask your victim to recite them—*again without writing.* There are 24: ABCD, ABDC, ACBD, ACDB, ADBC, ADCB, BACD, BADC, BCAD, BCDA, BDAC, BDCA, CABD, CADB, CBAD, CBDA, CDAB, CDBA, DABC, DACB, DBAC, DBCA, DCAB, and DCBA. (Note that the pattern is basically the same as three factorial, above; but in each set of six there is one more step.) Reciting the 24 combinations of A, B, C, and D is almost impossible, no matter how long one tries. *But with a pencil and paper most people can list them in less than four minutes.*

That experiment illustrates an important point about the human brain. The brain as an isolated organ has a surprising limitation: All of us can examine both combinations of A and B. But only about one out of five or six intelligent adults can give all six combinations of A, B, and C. And practically nobody can recite the 24 possible combinations of A, B, C, and D. **Using his or her brain alone, the average intelligent adult is capable of examining all possible combinations of between only two and three ideas—even when those ideas are as simple as A, B, and C.**

But when you use a pencil and paper—in other words, when the brain can *see* the ideas as it tries to arrange them, there is a dramatic increase in the number of concepts it can examine intelligently.

When you try to recite the 24 possible combinations of A, B, C, and D without looking at them, you are forcing your brain to operate as an isolated organ. But it is not an isolated organ. Only when the brain receives input through the senses—and especially the eyes—does it function as the world's most magnificent computer.

Seeing has no advantage over hearing as an input to the brain. But the written word has a major advantage over the spoken word. Written words stay, allowing you to examine and reexamine them; spoken words exist only the split second they are spoken. For this reason, you will always be able to do your best thinking when you jot the ideas on a piece of paper.

The Importance of the FALSE START

What does this have to do with your getting started? **Most people have trouble getting started, as we said before, because they are conscientiously trying to start correctly. But to figure out the best way to start, you must examine more than just the beginning. You must examine beginning, middle, and end— and all possible combinations of the ideas—to decide what is the *best* combination.** When you are sitting there, staring at a blank piece of paper until the deadline comes, you are trying to do that mentally, without being able to see the ideas.

However, we have shown with the A-B-C experiment that you probably are not capable of doing that. Your memory is not good enough. Your brain needs to SEE the ideas to be able to arrange them intelligently. No wonder you flounder trying to get started when you try to organize the ideas mentally!

What does the deadline change? Until the last moment, you were trying to start correctly. But starting correctly means planning the order of the ideas first, and we have already shown that you cannot do that mentally. It is physiologically impossible; the brain needs something to *look* at. Unable to be productive, you keep putting it off. Finally, the deadline demands that you start writing something, even if it is wrong. For the first time, you force yourself to put something down on paper—perhaps grudgingly. AND THEN: As you read what you have written, even if it is in the wrong order, your eyes begin feeding information to the brain the way the brain must receive it. You can then literally SEE what should have been the correct order.

This dramatizes one of the most important points in all of writing: *The false start is the necessary first step.*

If your report contains as many as three ideas, and if they are at least as complicated as A, B, and C, you cannot mentally examine all of the possible combinations. But when you are trying to start correctly, that is exactly what you are trying to do. **Only when the deadline comes, you get desperate enough to say "I've got to get started or I'm in trouble. At this point, any report is better than none. If it's wrong, I'll correct it later."**

So you start writing, conceding that what comes out will probably be pretty confused. **As the writing progresses, you are creating that false start—something for your brain to look at and correct.** Then, at some point you can **see** the proper order, and how you should have organized the writing in the first place. You then simply reorganize what you have written.

But you waste time that way. There is the delay of staring at the blank page. And there is all of the wasted work—yours and the typist's—in writing, then organizing, then rewriting. **Yet, that FALSE START—getting something down on paper so you can look at it and correct it—is the necessary first step.** There must be a way to make that false start at the beginning, without all the delay, and without the need of writing the report the wrong way and then rewriting it. Of course, there is such a way. What are we leading up to? THE OUTLINE.

Well, there is the hated word. Outline, outline, outline! It is the most important single step in writing—whether you are writing a business letter, an engineering report, or the great American novel.

Yes, novelists outline too. Perhaps the popular impression is that the novelist sits down at a typewriter and fills page one, then plans what will happen on page two, and so on, filling wastebaskets as he or she progresses. No, no. The novelist first develops the plot carefully in outline form. This is called the *'plotline.'* Only when the story is completed in plotline form—from beginning to end in great detail—does he or she begin expanding it into words and sentences. In fact, Ernest Hemingway wrote about this in his advice to young writers. He said that the plotline or outline determines the success of the writing. It is here that you determine whether or not you will win literary awards. The outline (plotline), Hemingway said, is the architecture of writing; words and sentences are just the interior decoration.

Notice Hemingway is acknowledging that great writing depends first on valuable, well-planned ideas—and only then on the writer's skill at choosing words and building them into sentences. It is no different when you are writing a business letter or report.

(By the way, have you noticed where the conclusion came in this session of *Put It In Writing*? The conclusion, or overview, is that you must outline before you write. And we led up to it gradually. Why? Remember, Session 4 emphasized that the conclusion should normally go at the beginning, *unless it is so unpleasant it would close the reader's mind to the reasons.* Outlining is certainly that unpopular; most people do not want to read or hear anything about it. So we deliberately built up gradually to that conclusion, to avoid the risk of losing your interest at the beginning of Session 5. This is the only time we have done that in this course.)

Outline before you write. The brain—magnificent computer that it is—simply is not good enough to organize ideas without looking at them first. *The false start is the necessary first step!*

Infamous Quotation No. 2

U.S. education has been under severe criticism since the 1970's for failing to teach basic skills. English teachers have been particularly singled out as writing skills have declined. But not all English teachers agree they should teach writing.

At a conference on career education in Cleveland, Ohio in 1979, a high school English teacher said (and his colleagues agreed): "My job is to teach literature, not writing. I resent the implication that we should spend precious classroom time so students can go out and write engineering or business reports. That's vocational education, and I'm not a voc ed teacher."

(Also see: *Infamous Quotation No. 1,* page 17.)

How to Outline:
Sense and Nonsense

Most people, when they finally do admit they must outline, put in the upper left hand corner: Roman Numeral I. Then what? They sit and stare at **that** for days.

No Roman Numerals, please. At least, not yet.

Remember, the first purpose of the outline is to allow yourself the luxury of the *false start*—quickly, and with little wasted effort. **When you put Roman Numeral I at the top of the page, you have deprived yourself of that false start. Truly, you are worse off than when the page was bare. You have now committed yourself to writing first things first, second things second, etc.** Before you could write them that way, however, you would have to think them that way. But we have already shown with the A-B-C experiment that you cannot think the proper order of the ideas unless you can see them.

The only sensible first outline is that FALSE START. The first outline is going to be wrong—something to look at and correct. Simply throw ideas down on the page in random order. Imagine you tilt your head forward and let the ideas spill out onto the page. Use key word phrases. Do not give any consideration at this point to proper order, or even to separating major from minor ideas. Just throw down a random list, almost like a pile of building materials from which you are going to plan the structure of your letter or report. *And that structure will be: an Inverted Pyramid.*

Once you have that random list before you—and it can be very rough—your brain has something it can look at. Then, from that point on you will find you can organize intelligently, because the brain will take over as a computer. Now you will be able to see the relationships as they should be. You will start drawing arrows back and forth, or by some other method rearrange the order of the ideas. Use whatever method best suits your work habits. Examine one arrangement, then another, until you finally arrive at the one that seems best.

Remember, last session we examined how to structure a letter or report— probably as an Inverted Pyramid, with the conclusion at the beginning. It is at this point, when you have put down your random list of ideas and are now sitting looking at them, that you can plan that structure intelligently—in skeleton form.

You will probably be pleasantly surprised. This really works. Rearrange the ideas in skeleton form. Examine one arrangement, then another, until you have finally arrived at the one that best suits you. Then, incidentally, you can add the Roman Numerals, if you wish. They may help the reader by showing degrees of subordination. But they can cause you, the writer, considerable harm in the early planning unless you put them in *after you have outlined*.

THESE TWO SIMPLE RULES SHOULD HELP YOU TO OUTLINE:

Use a piece of scrap paper. Remember, the first version must be a FALSE START. Perhaps it should be on a sheet of paper having heel marks or coffee rings, to remind you: If it does not end in the wastebasket in a few minutes, you are not using it correctly. It should be something just to look at and correct.

Use key word phrases. Do not write the ideas in full sentences. You should not yet be thinking about picking the right words or building them into the best possible sentences. That comes later.

Outlining is easy. At least, that first step, the false start, should be—just putting down your random list of key word phrases. But then, structuring them into one carefully planned and intelligently related group of ideas may be the hardest part of the entire job. After all, it is here that you will do your major thinking. It is here that you will establish the logical relationships between your ideas. It is here, in other words, that you will establish the *intelligence* and therefore the *value* and ultimate success of what you write.

Therefore, outlining is surely the most important single step in any writing.

Outlining improves your word/sentence skill. Surprisingly, by outlining you will also do a better job of selecting words and building them into sentences later, when you are finally ready for them. Why? Because, **while outlining you will be dividing writing into its two major elements—*what* you write and *how* you write it—and concentrating on them separately.** Or, as we have been telling you since this course began, you will be making that vital separation between your *ideas* and the *words and sentences* with which you convey them.

Plan the ideas intelligently in the outline first. Only then are you ready to begin working to express them fully in words and sentences. **If you will separate the work this way, you will be better at both parts of it, because you can concentrate on each separately, without diverting energy into the other. Your ideas will be more intelligently thought out, and your words and sentences will probably be clearer and more eloquent.**

Trying to write without an outline is like trying to build a house without blueprints. If you finish with something of quality, it will be either by accident or through much ripping apart and rebuilding.

Give yourself a road map to follow before leaving on the writing trip. Without an outline, everything is likely to go wrong. The structure of the writing suffers because you tend to report the ideas in the order you lived them—or worse, in no order at all. Your words and sentences suffer also, because you are too busy untangling the ideas to pay much attention to expressing them the clearest possible way. And you waste time correcting mistakes on rough drafts instead of making and correcting them in skeleton form.

How long should it take? Outlining may be the hardest part of writing in some cases. But it is surely the most important part. Forget the notion that outlining is a five-minute job. It may take five minutes, or it may take three-quarters of your total writing time. **In general, a 1:1 ratio may be a reasonable guide; plan on spending as much time outlining as writing.** For most people, that would mean reproportioning the writing time—more time planning, less time writing. **You will usually save time.** But more important, the finished product is likely to be better organized and better written.

How detailed should it be? Only you can decide. Certainly, any useful outline must contain all of your *major* ideas—the ones that would have *Roman Numerals* in a traditional outline. How far you plan the outline beyond that is mostly a matter of your own personal work habits. One thing we can assure you: The more detailed the outline, the easier, better organized, and more clearly written will be the finished writing.

Acronyms: Mercy to Your Reader

An acronym is a word made of the initials of a complex name or special term. Used properly, acronyms are acts of kindness to your reader; they replace difficult terms with simple ones.

But they are simple only if known. Therefore, always spell out the full term the first time it appears in any piece of writing; then follow it immediately by the acronym in parentheses, almost as if saying, "...hereinafter referred to as...." Example: *Pump output is measured in gallons per minute (GPM).*

Warning: Don't overuse acronyms. If a sentence or a page looks like a bowl of alphabet soup *(The CPHM reading in the WRG indicates a PNA and should be acted upon by the SOD....),* you are being inconsiderate, not merciful, to your reader.

Guidelines for Nonsexist Writing

Avoiding sexist language is not only morally correct, it is easy. In some writing, it is also the law.

English is notoriously sexist—more so than any other major language, according to language scholars. Still, it is possible to write **anything** without sexist references of any kind, if you are willing. Furthermore, doing so should not make your writing any more difficult, and it need not create the least bit of awkward wording.

The infamous generic *he*.

This is, of course, the most common abuse. For years business people have written statements like: *The reader may not be aware he misunderstood.* Unthinkable today. So you write: *The reader may not be aware he/she misunderstood.* At least, it will avoid complaints. But it is awkward. It calls attention to itself, especially if you do it often.

One simple change will get rid of three quarters of those sexist statements—graciously. *He* and *she* are **third person** pronouns. English simply does not have third person neutral personal pronouns **in the singular**. Switch, then, to **plural**: *Readers may not be aware they misunderstood.* Or, switch to second person: *You may not be aware. . . .* (You should do that anyhow, where it fits, in writing that addresses the reader directly. Your writing will be warmer, a desirable trait.)

That type of change will usually work, but not always. For example, in a memo to supervisors you might write: *The supervisor must inform an employee as soon as he or she is suspected of drug abuse that he or she may face disciplinary action.* Second person *(inform you . . . that you may face)* will not work here if the writing is addressed to someone else. Plural *(inform employees . . . that they may face)* will not work in situations that refer to one person. So you must use the *he or she*—even if the sentence requires it twice, as here. This usage is awkward only if you use it repeatedly. And use *he* or *she* rather than *he/she*. It sounds better to the mind's ear.

Job descriptions, one of the curses of anybody who has ever tried to write them, are a bit harder to keep nonsexist, but still not very hard. Here, more than in most other kinds of writing, old-fashioned (sexist) language habits are an invitation to legal difficulties. Federal courts have ruled that all-male policy statements, even though unintentional, are discriminatory, and some companies have been hurt by resulting law suits.

The problem in job descriptions is that you are writing a series of required skills or duties (or both) for *any* employee who holds that particular job, and each sentence tends to have a pronoun (traditionally *he*) as its subject:

The (job title) must be capable of reading and understanding blueprints according to NA level 6 specifications. He must be capable of making bookkeeping entries and preparing financial statements in NCPA format. He must . . . . He must. . . .

Unacceptable. That invites Equal Employment Opportunity grievances. *You* or *they* will not work here. Using *he or she* each time will quickly become distracting, and the style awkward. Combining several statements into fewer longer sentences would mean fewer subjects, therefore fewer sexist/nonsexist word choices. But such sentences quickly become too long and complex for inexperienced employees to follow.

Solution: Write each section of a job description as a series of phrases, without subjects. This can be done in correct grammar and in smooth, gracious style.

For each section, an introductory phrase contains the subject; this is followed by a series of sentence fragments, each without a subject, each telling one of the requirements. **Example:**

The (job title) must be capable of:
—reading and understanding blueprints according to
NA level 6 specifications.
—making bookkeeping entries and preparing financial
statements in NCPA format.

Be sure to list the ideas vertically, indented, as they are here. That way they can be read separately, rather than as one unbearably long sentence, even though grammatically they are still one sentence. Changes of this kind are easy and will avoid Equal Employment Opportunity grievances. Caution: this format can tend to sound choppy and fragmented; therefore, take extra care to be smooth.

Other *man* words.

With equal ease you can get rid of all other *man* words. They are never, never necessary. *Man is a social animal* . . . . would be better as, *People are social animals.* Anthropologically, both statements say exactly the same thing. *Since the beginning of mankind* . . . . would be better as, *Since the earliest human history.* . . . . In both cases, the nonsexist version is clear, gracious, and just as accurate.

Male bosses and female secretaries?

That may indeed be the situation in most offices, but you must not portray it that way in your writing. You lose no effectiveness whatever in an interoffice memo or letter by writing, *Every executive must be aware of his or her responsibilities.* . . . Or, of course, *Every secretary must be aware of his or her.* . . . Incredibly, the National Council for Teachers of English (NCTE) recommends . . . *must be aware of their.* . . . That is terrible grammar, however (singular noun, plural pronoun), and unnecessary. Once poor grammar is endorsed for special situations, where does it stop? Who decides if a situation is special enough? This academic permissiveness is an invitation to the "anything goes" attitude in language usage. Some NCTE committees endorse that attitude.

Avoid job titles that identify sex. *Mailmen* have become mail *carriers. Salesmen* are *sales representatives.* In airplanes, *stewardesses* have become *flight attendants.* Likewise, if you are seriously interested in finding nonsexist descriptions in your writing, you surely can without much effort.

What about *chairman?* No mystery. Use *chairman* for males, *chairwoman* for females. If it is a theoretical one, use *presiding officer,* or *committee head,* or even *person in charge.* Please do **not** use the grossly distasteful "chair," which is also recommended by NCTE.

Never refer to a grown woman as a girl. *The girl who took the order* . . . . will get you icy stares, and should. *The woman who took the order* . . . . is far more thoughtful. Also, never refer to women as *ladies.* The word is judgmental, and people who care about these matters insist such judgment is not necessary.

About *Ms.*

Yes, you should use it in addressing all women—single or married. We do not have different forms of *Mr.* for single and married men. According to surveys, the word *Ms.* (pronounced *mizz*) has slowly but consistently gained in popularity. By the late 1970's, most professional women favored it, and most publishers' style manuals endorsed it. *(The United States Government Printing Office Style Manual,* however, stayed mum on this subject. *The Chicago Manual of Style* acknowledges the use of *Ms.* but does not encourage or discourage its use.)

The Hippopotamus Joke

The zoo manager was about to be fired. The trouble was that the zoo needed two hippopotamuses, but he kept putting off ordering them because he didn't know whether to say "hippopotamuses" or "hippopotami."

When you get desperate enough, you often find a way, and he did. On the last desperate day he wrote the hippopotamus company (or wherever you buy hippopotamuses): "Gentlemen, Will you please send to the undersigned one healthy adult hippopotamus." He signed his name, then added: "P.S.—as long as you're sending one, make it two."

Moral: There is a right way of saying anything, but you usually don't find it by piling more junk on the wrong way.

(Also see: The *Penguin Joke,* page 11.)

(Also see *Salutations, Gentlemen,* page 108.)

• •

Why do most intelligent adults have trouble getting started on major writing jobs?

They try to put it together (organize it) in their heads.

The brain has a surprising limitation that affects your ability to organize ideas. Please describe it.

Needs to visually see ideas

Most people do their best writing only at the deadline. Why? What does the deadline force you to do differently?

Start writing something (false start) in order to meet deadline

The *false* *Start* *is the necessary first step in writing.*

As a guide, what proportion of your total writing time should you reasonably expect to spend outlining?

45-50% - Closer to 50%

What is the objection to using Roman Numerals as you begin outlining?

Puts you back to square one - Doesn't allow for false start

How will outlining improve your ability to pick the right words and build them into clear, precise sentences?

While outlining you divide writing into the how and what.

Outlining will almost always save you time. True or false? *True*

What is the easy way to avoid using 'he' to refer to both sexes?

they - use plural

How can you avoid using 'chair,' without being sexist?

Chairman/Chairwoman

SESSION 5
Exercise

EXERCISE 21.

Outlining is the most important single step in writing. It is here that you determine everything of value in your letter or report. But a FALSE START is the necessary first step, because the brain can arrange ideas logically only when it can see them. Therefore a random list of the ideas should be the first step in outlining. (Most people make that false start by writing the report in the wrong order, then rewriting it.)

Imagine that you are going to write a report on the subject of flextime, a policy many companies and government agencies are adopting, which allows employees to choose their own working hours. You have just listed all the ideas you can think of on the subject, in random order as they came into your head. That list appears below; it is your false start:

1	Reduces absenteeism and tardiness	1	Reduces cafeteria congestion
2	Scheduling is difficult	3	Hewlett Packard
4	Rules printed and distributed	4	Coordinator must be appointed
1	Increases personal freedom	1	Makes personnel recruitment easier
4	Objectives must be defined	3	Department of Transportation
4	Management support needed	1	Reduced parking congestion
2	Slows down communications	3	Metropolitan Life Insurance
1	Improves public image	4	Employee briefing needed
2	Hourly employees may complain	1	Reduces turnover
3	Smith Kline Corporation	3	U.S. Department of Agriculture
1	Raises employee morale	4	Hours must be limited
		2	Expands hours dealers can phone us

(Continued on next page)

EXERCISE 21 (Continued)

As you examine the random list (previous page), you begin to **see** relationships you could not envision before. The ideas clearly fall into four categories. Those categories are:

Your Version

1 ADVANTAGES
2 DISADVANTAGES
3 USERS OF FLEX TIME
~~Objectives~~
4 IMPLEMENTATION or
           STEPS TO BE Taken IN
                ADVANCE

Course Recommends

EXERCISE 21 (Continued)

Now outline the rest of the report. List those four main categories by order of importance; then under each one list the minor ideas. Only then are you ready to write the report, expanding the ideas fully into words and sentences. (But you need not write the whole thing.) After you have outlined, the hardest work is done.

• •

I _____

_____

_____

_____

_____

Your Outline

II _____

_____

_____

_____

_____

III _____

_____

_____

_____

_____

IV _____

_____

_____

_____

_____

(Continued on next page)

EXERCISE 21 (Continued)

The four main categories by order of importance, with the minor ideas listed under each one:

Course Recommends

I _____

_____

_____

_____

_____

II _____

_____

_____

_____

_____

III _____

_____

_____

_____

_____

IV _____

_____

_____

_____

_____

(Continued on next page)

EXERCISE 21 (Continued)

Now, as you examine those four major categories, you should begin to see things about them that you could not see before. Does one of the major ideas stand out? Or does some new idea suggest itself? Perhaps now you can see what your **overview** statement should be. (Remember, the Inverted Pyramid demands that you start with the one statement or group of statements that sums up the whole report.)

In the imaginary report on page 93, what would be your opening statement, or overview? It can be more than one sentence:

Your Version

Implementing flex time has many advantages for both the company and the employee. Although it has it's drawbacks, many companies like Smith Klene & H. P. have ~~solved~~ addressed these issues.

Course Recommends

EXERCISE 22.

Usually you can avoid sexist references by switching to the plural, changing *'he'* to *'they'*. But that doesn't always work. Sometimes you can avoid needing any pronoun at all, by slight rewording of the phrase containing it. Other times, you may find that *'he or she'* is just right.

The passage below is thoughtful and courteous—to men. A few word changes in each sentence will make the whole passage nonsexist:

Invite ~~the~~ new employee to contribute *their* ~~his~~ talent to the department's daily operations. Encourage ~~him~~ *them* to come to you ~~if he has any~~ *with* questions. Every new employee should be made to feel ~~that his~~ *the importance of* contribution ~~is important~~ to the company.

Your Rewrite

_____

_____

_____

_____

_____

_____

_____

_____

Course Recommends

_____

_____

_____

_____

_____

_____

_____

_____

EXERCISE 23.

Nonsexist language may require a new way of choosing words—especially if you're male. But it is always possible if you are willing. Futhermore, it does not require any extra work. A few slight changes to this male-oriented (but otherwise charming) social commentary will make it acceptable to everyone:

As he progressed from caveman to nuclear warrior, man's needs became more complex. Animal skins were once adequate body covering; now he needs business suits, jeans, and tuxedos. Campfire rituals were once adequate recreation; now he invents football. Once, a father needed to provide only food and protection. Occasionally, the chairman ~~third~~ of the board can be forgiven for pausing to wonder: Am I any happier than that caveman?

Your Rewrite

As we progressed from cave dwellers
citizens of the age, people needs
to nuclear warriors, ~~we became~~ needs
became more complex. Animal skins
were once adequate body coverings; now
we need business attire, jeans and formal
wear. Campfire rituals were once adequate
recreation; now we have invented sports.
Once a

Course Recommends

**"The great enemy
of clear language
is insecurity."**

—George Orwell

The Finishing Touches of the Pros

A few simple mechanical things can help your reader by making the pages easy to read. These are perhaps the last five percent of your work. Sometimes a writer takes great pains to organize well and write clearly, only to ruin the effect by not doing these simple things correctly. The last 5 percent of the job ruins the other 95 percent.

Headings: Readers Love Them

Probably the most important of mechanical considerations is the use of headings. They are easy to use, and they immediately add a touch of professionalism. Consider using headings in all reports. The longer the report, the more helpful they are to the reader. (But do not use them in letters. They make a letter look like a form letter, and readers resent that.)

Headings help the reader three ways. First, they provide overviews along the way; they announce key points *before* the details. Remember, the reader understands the details better knowing in advance what he or she is going to receive. **Second, they help the reader to read selectively**—choosing some passages but not others. **And third, headings give the reader places to stop temporarily, to regroup the thoughts or to rest.**

Headings will also help you, the writer, by relieving you of the need to write transition passages. They provide all the transition you need. They allow you to flow smoothly and easily from the end of one major idea to the beginning of the next.

A good outline tells what your headings should be and where they should go. Just take those key word phrases from your finished, carefully planned outline and deposit them into the report. You will be pleasantly surprised how easy and effective they are.

The Importance of White Space

The next thing you can do to improve the appearance and readability of your writing is to use plenty of white space. It is easy to use, inexpensive, and effective. Many conscientious typists tend to squeeze too much on a page, robbing you of white space. Do not let them. **Insist on at least an inch of white space at major headings, to make them stand out.** Remember, those headings should be immediately noticeable to the scanning reader.

Also, tell the typist to leave at least one inch of white space around all four sides of every sheet that ever leaves the typewriter. **Any good secretarial manual says margins should be at least one inch wide.** Be sure they are.

Also, be sure the typist skips a line between paragraphs. If a letter is double-spaced, it should be triple-spaced between paragraphs. There should be a visible gap at the paragraph breaks. This is especially important as indented paragraphs are becoming obsolete in letters (or other typewritten material).

You must control these things. The typist has a tendency to try to save paper. This is admirable, but there is something far more important than the cost of paper: the cost and the effectiveness of the ideas that go on it.

Paragraph Structuring

Paragraphs help the reader two ways. First, they present clusters of related sentences; therefore, they are important building blocks in your logic. Second, and less commonly known, paragraphs provide eye muscle relief. The breaks allow the reader to glance from the page for a split second and then find his or her place quickly.

How long should paragraphs be? Generally, like sentences, keep them short. Look for places to break them. **Your paragraphs probably should average about seven or eight lines. But also like sentences, a good mixture is desirable—minimum one line, maximum 15. Let the size and shape of the cluster of sentences determine the size and shape of the paragraph.**

Reading experts point out that comprehension begins to drop after about 10 typewritten lines and drops drastically after about 15 lines. (Curiously, this is true regardless of the width of the lines.) If there is no logical breaking point after about 15 lines in your writing, break anyhow.

Each paragraph does *not* require a topic sentence. You may have learned that it does, but that is too rigid a discipline.

Also, it is *not* true that a paragraph must contain more than one sentence. In fact, an effective way to emphasize an idea is to write it as a very short sentence and make it a separate paragraph. It practically jumps off the page. Do not do this very often, however.

Here you see a sample of a page that is set up thoughtfully for the consideration of the reader. It uses headings, and white space at the paragraph breaks:

(See next page)

THE QUESTION MARK

People know how to use question marks properly; you end questions with them, as you end sentences with periods.

The trouble is, most writers don't use questions in their writing. Why not? They are as useful in writing as in speech, and there is little reason to deprive yourself of them.

THE EXCLAMATION POINT

Most writers should not need the exclamation point very often. But when you need it, how marvelously it performs! An exclamation point is a period with a bang. Not much of a bang, but enough that it signals to the reader that the writer wanted emphasis here.

QUOTATION MARKS

Generally speaking, use them only for quotations. Do not use them unless you are repeating the exact words of the person being quoted. Always use them in pairs. Use single quotation marks for a quotation within a quotation. (On most typewriters the apostrophe is used for this.)

We say *generally speaking* because some writers use quotation marks another way—not for quotations but to notify the reader that a word or phrase is being used in some unusual way: *The air seemed "stuffy" after the storm.* The writer seems almost to be apologizing for using the word. This usage of quotation marks is controversial, but most language authorities tolerate it. A wise attitude might be: If you have to apologize very often for using words, you're probably not using them very well.

THE HYPHEN

Use hyphens to divide words that won't fit at the end of a line. Here, a bit of common sense is called for. Breaking a word this way is generally undesirable, and if you can avoid breaking one by lengthening (or shortening) a line by a few letters, you should do so. If you must divide, do so only between syllables (indicated in dictionaries by a dot between letters).

Use hyphens also to connect the words of a compound adjective if the absence of the hyphen could cause misunderstanding: *The model 4000 comes complete with four-channel indicators* (indicators with four channels). There is a great difference between that and: *The model 4000 comes complete with four channel indicators* (four indicators of channels). Compound adjectives may be more than two words: *Ready-to-wear clothing, faster-than-average production rate, seventy-six-year-old marathon runner.*

Notice how easy the information is to read with headings, and how attractive and professional they make the pages look.

To demonstrate the importance of headings, here is that same passage without them—with white space where the headings were before:

People know how to use question marks properly; you end questions with them, as you end sentences with periods.

The trouble is, most writers don't use questions in their writing. Why not? They are as useful in writing as in speech, and there is little reason to deprive yourself of them.

Most writers should not need the exclamation point very often. But when you need it, how marvelously it performs! An exclamation point is a period with a bang. Not much of a bang, but enough that it signals to the reader that the writer wanted emphasis here.

Generally speaking, use quotation marks only for quotations. Do not use them unless you are repeating the exact words of the person being quoted. Always use them in pairs. Use single quotation marks for a quotation within a quotation. (On most typewriters the apostrophe is used for this.)

We say *generally speaking* because some writers use quotation marks another way—not for quotations but to notify the reader that a word or phrase is being used in some unusual way: *The air seemed "stuffy" after the storm.* The writer seems almost to be apologizing for using the word. This usage of quotation marks is controversial, but most language authorities tolerate it. A wise attitude might be: If you have to apologize very often for using words, you're probably not using them very well.

Use hyphens to divide words that won't fit at the end of a line. Here, a bit of common sense is called for. Breaking a word this way is generally undesirable, and if you can avoid breaking one by lengthening (or shortening) a line by a few letters, you should do so. If you must divide, do so only between syllables (indicated in dictionaries by a dot between letters).

Use hyphens also to connect the words of a compound adjective if the absence of the hyphen could cause misunderstanding: *The model 4000 comes complete with four-channel indicators* (indicators with four channels). There is a great difference between that and: *The model 4000 comes complete with four channel indicators* (four indicators of channels). Compound adjectives may be more than two words: *Ready-to-wear clothing, faster-than-average production rate, seventy-six-year-old marathon runner.*

Here is the same passage with the headings but with no white space. Notice that the overview statements and paragraph breaks are there, but they are lost to the scanning reader:

THE QUESTION MARK
People know how to use question marks properly; you end questions with them, as you end sentences with periods.

The trouble is, most writers don't use questions in their writing. Why not? They are as useful in writing as in speech, and there is little reason to deprive yourself of them.

THE EXCLAMATION POINT
Most writers should not need the exclamation point very often. But when you need it, how marvelously it performs! An exclamation point is a period with a bang. Not much of a bang, but enough that it signals to the reader that the writer wanted emphasis here.

QUOTATION MARKS
Generally speaking, use them only for quotations. Do not use them unless you are repeating the exact words of the person being quoted. Always use them in pairs. Use single quotation marks for a quotation within a quotation. (On most typewriters the apostrophe is used for this.)

We say *generally speaking* because some writers use quotation marks another way—not for quotations but to notify the reader that a word or phrase is being used in some unusual way: *The air seemed "stuffy" after the storm.* The writer seems almost to be apologizing for using the word. This usage of quotation marks is controversial, but most language authorities tolerate it. A wise attitude might be: If you have to apologize very often for using words, you're probably not using them very well.

THE HYPHEN
Use hyphens to divide words that won't fit at the end of a line. Here, a bit of common sense is called for. Breaking a word this way is generally undesirable, and if you can avoid breaking one by lengthening (or shortening) a line by a few letters, you should do so. If you must divide, do so only between syllables (indicated in dictionaries by a dot between letters).

Use hyphens also to connect the words of a compound adjective if the absence of the hyphen could cause misunderstanding: *The model 4000 comes complete with four-channel indicators* (indicators with four channels). There is a great difference between that and: *The model 4000 comes complete with four channel indicators* (four indicators of channels). Compound adjectives may be more than two words: *Ready-to-wear clothing, faster-than-average production rate, seventy-six-year-old marathon runner.*

Here is the same information again, with neither white space nor headings—just one solid glob waiting for the reader:

People know how to use question marks properly; you end questions with them, as you end sentences with periods. The trouble is, most writers don't use questions in their writing. Why not? They are as useful in writing as in speech, and there is little reason to deprive yourself of them. Most writers should not need the exclamation point very often. But when you need it, how marvelously it performs! An exclamation point is a period with a bang. Not much of a bang, but enough that it signals to the reader that the writer wanted emphasis here. Generally speaking, use quotation marks only for quotations. Do not use them unless you are repeating the exact words of the person being quoted. Always use them in pairs. Use single quotation marks for a quotation within a quotation. (On most typewriters the apostrophe is used for this.) We say *generally speaking* because some writers use quotation marks another way—not for quotations but to notify the reader that a word or phrase is being used in some unusual way: *The air seemed "stuffy" after the storm.* The writer seems almost to be apologizing for using the word. This usage of quotation marks is controversial, but most language authorities tolerate it. A wise attitude might be: If you have to apologize very often for using words, you're probably not using them very well. Use hyphens to divide words that won't fit at the end of a line. Here, a bit of common sense is called for. Breaking a word this way is generally undesirable, and if you can avoid breaking one by lengthening (or shortening) a line by a few letters, you should do so. If you must divide, do so only between syllables (indicated in dictionaries by a dot between letters). Use hyphens also to connect the words of a compound adjective if the absence of the hyphen could cause misunderstanding: *The model 4000 comes complete with four-channel indicators* (indicators with four channels). There is a great difference between that and: *The model 4000 comes complete with four channel indicators* (four indicators of channels). Compound adjectives may be more than two words: *Ready-to-wear clothing, faster-than-average production rate, seventy-six-year-old marathon runner.* Three spaced dots (and you should instruct the typist to put spaces between them) in a quotation tell the reader you have deliberately left out some of the words: *Abraham Lincoln said, "My paramount objective . . . is to save the union, and is not either to save or destroy slavery."* A little-known (and not very important) fact about ellipses: Three dots indicate the omission of words *in the middle* of a sentence. Four dots indicate that the omission continues *to the end* of a sentence; the fourth dot stands for the period.

Never present information that way to your reader. It is thoughtless and inconsiderate. The reader gets discouraged just seeing that coming.

Where Should Graphics Go?

Graphs, charts, tables, drawings, photographs, and other forms of graphics are often vital—especially in reports. How you present them is important to your reader, and that is mostly a matter of *where* you position them.

In a very short report (perhaps one to three pages), simply add them as attachments at the end, the same as you would if they were enclosures with a business letter.

But in a long report, never force your reader to go elsewhere to understand what he or she is reading, if you can avoid it. Usually you can. **Put each graph, table, etc., in the body of the report—right on the page where you are discussing it, if possible.** Put them in an Appendix only when there are so many graphics they would break up the report badly if they were interspersed throughout, or when they are definitely unimportant (optional) reading.

Also, be sure to write a full, detailed caption for each graphic. Do not presume your readers can examine your graphics as intelligently as you can. In fact, you should probably presume the opposite. After all, **you** are the expert in your field; **you** probably developed that graph, chart, or table and are intimately familiar with the information it contains. This caption should be an overview statement—a brief summary of the graphic. It may be as long as four or five lines. It should tell enough that the reader can learn the highlights of the graph, chart, or table without studying it in detail and without reading about it in the body. This means you are doing some repeating, but only of key information. The graphic and its caption should be capable of standing alone, fully self-explanatory.

Ways To Add Emphasis

Smart writers occasionally single out key words or short passages for emphasis. Try it if you are not accustomed to doing so. After all, when we talk we instinctively raise or lower our voice, or gesture with our hands, or pause to emphasize key ideas to our listener. You can—and should—do a few simple things to achieve those same results for your reader.

Some useful methods are underlining, capital letters, boldface type, or italics.

In the past, typewriters offered only <u>underlining</u> or CAPITAL LETTERS; only commercial printers could use **boldface type** or *italics*. Today almost every word processor can give you boldface type, and if you have a laser printer italics are also possible.

Use bullets (dots at the beginnings of lines or paragraphs) to emphasize several ideas presented consecutively as a series.

All of these devices are used throughout this Manual—and in other books and magazines you have been reading all your life. It is surprising, however, how many business writers overlook taking advantage of these marvelously useful tools. Do not overuse them, however, or the effect is lost.

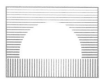

Fact and Fancy About Letters

All of the advice of this course on clarity and structure applies to letters as much as to any other kind of writing. Only a few things about letters are different from other kinds of writing, and those few things are purely mechanical.

The Address Block. Include in this order: name; title; department (if you name one); company; street address; city, state, and zip code. Notice that the name of the person you are writing ordinarily belongs on the first line, not in an attention line at the bottom of the address block. Commonly, the attention line is used only when sending legal or financial documents.

The Subject Line. Do you need one? It may be useful. But do not use a subject line unless your company or department requires it, or you feel it serves some specific purpose. If it is required, it may benefit one of two people: the boss who scans outgoing mail, or the file clerk. But notice they are both at the sending end. Your subject line is usually of no value to anyone at the receiving end. Therefore, two rules are important for subject lines if you use them at all:

First: Keep them short. We said subject *line,* not paragraph. If this line gets longer than a few words, the file clerk gets different choices of subjects to file under, and the boss loses the chance to scan quickly to decide which letters to read.

Second: Never refer to the subject line in the body of the letter. Doing so would penalize the reader by making him or her look two different places for the information. This means you may never refer to the *'above subject study,'* or the *'above subject equipment,'* or the above subject anything.

The Salutation. Somehow, people manage so often to use the wrong one. Use the name of the person you are writing if you know it: *'Dear Mr. Wilton.'* And by the way, it is perfectly proper to address a person by first name in a dignified business letter—if you would normally do so face to face. Never use *'Dear Sir'* or *'Gentlemen.'* If you are writing to a person by title but do not have that person's name (formerly the *'Dear Sir'* situation), use the title as a salutation: *'Dear Sales Manager,'* or *'Dear Research Director.'* If you have neither a name nor a title (formerly the *'Gentlemen'* situation), *'Dear Reader'* seems to be the best the experts have been able to recommend. *'Dear Sir or Madam'* or *'Gentlepersons'* just will not do. English is notoriously sexist, and even though we may want to change we sometimes do not have the right word. One suggestion: A simple phone call to a switchboard operator or secretary will usually give you the information you need for a more specific and courteous salutation.

The various salutations are not interchangeable. With a little thought, it should be easy to use the right one.

Incidentally, people often question the use of the word *'Dear'* at the beginning of the salutation. You may drop it if you like. Most readers will not even notice it is missing if the rest of the letter is warm and courteous. And of course, if the letter is cold, *'Dear'* will not make it warmer. But do not drop the entire salutation—just the word *'Dear.'* Also, avoid using off-beat salutations like *'Good morning Mr. Wilton,'* etc.

What salutation is appropriate when you are not sure whether you are writing a man or woman? Find out. Again, a simple phone call will usually give you the information you need for an accurate and courteous salutation.

And what to do if you know it is a woman but are unsure whether she is *'Miss'* or *'Mrs.'?* Use the salutation *'Ms,'* (pronounced "Mizz'). In fact, you should probably use that for all women. It has gained respectability in recent years and, after all, we do not have separate titles for married and single men.

The Opening Sentence. Many people use a cliché opening. That is, some group of words used routinely to convey an implied meaning. People often use these automatically, as a substitute for thinking of an individual message for each letter. Such openings have all the sparkle of a bureaucratic form letter, and they make your letter sound like one. (Indeed, these clichés are most common in form letters, where the motive is often to be as general as possible so the same wording will fit as many situations as possible.)

Try to avoid opening sentences containing such standard clichés as *'in response to,'* or *'with reference to,'* or *'in accordance with,'* or *'relative to.'* They are dull and overworked, and suggest that you did not put much work or thought into your opening. They have all the interest of a rubber stamp, and create the impression that the writer is a rubber stamp with arms and legs (but no head). Here is an example of a typical cliché opening:

Mr. Matwood,

In response to your letter of February 19 relative to leasing office equipment, the Internal Revenue Service regulations on this point are complex. The technical differences between purchasing and leasing are not always clearly defined, and whether IRS considers your transaction a lease or purchase can be of tremendous importance in determining your tax rate.

Frankly, we doubt if there would be any advantage to. . . .

Here is that same letter, but this time opening with a thoughtful, original statement that applies specifically to this letter:

Mr. Matwood,

Thank you for your letter of February 19 questioning whether you should lease or buy office equipment.

The Internal Revenue Service regulations on this point are complex. The technical differences between purchasing and leasing are not always clearly defined, and whether IRS considers your transaction a lease or purchase can be of tremendous importance in determining your tax rate.

Frankly, we doubt if there would be any advantage to. . . .

People who defend those cliché openings do so on the grounds that the beginning should give a briefing of past correspondence. We are not opposed to that kind of briefing (although it is not always necessary). But, in fact, if you do want that briefing at the beginning, notice that the individually thought out opening gives a far better, more informative briefing than the automatic opening.

About Dictation

In terms of the quality of the finished writing, most business men and women write best when they do their own first draft—either in longhand or by typing their own. They do somewhat worse dictating to a secretary, and worst of all dictating to a machine. Why does dictation produce poor writing? It should not, and it need not. It is certainly the fastest way to write. And it makes possible conversational style, which would improve most people's writing. **The main trouble with dictation is that it deprives your brain of something to look at.**

Remember, we demonstrated in Section 5 with the A-B-C Experiment that it is impossible to organize your ideas well unless you can see them. Therefore, *outline first—even for the simplest letter—before you turn on the dictating machine.* Prepare for dictation by giving yourself a roadmap to follow before you leave on the verbal trip. Make sure you are through planning the order of the ideas before you begin the task of picking words and building them into sentences. Separating the two halves of the writing job that way—first the *what,* then the *how*—you will be better at both because you can give each your full attention. Your ideas will be better organized, **and your words and sentences will be stronger when you are finally ready to dictate them.**

Here is a piece of advice specifically for machine dictation. Learn how to use whatever method your machine has for making corrections. The typist would like to know in advance if there are corrections. Nothing upsets any typist more than doing a perfect letter, only to hear after finishing that you changed something. You must certainly have the right to make changes after you dictate. But let the typist know about them before typing. Dictating machines always provide some method of doing this.

Should you dictate punctuation, or let the secretary insert the punctuation marks? Generally, the writer knows better what effect he or she is trying to create with words and punctuation marks, and therefore should be better able to decide which ones should be used, and where they should go. The trouble is, secretaries usually know the rules of punctuation better. A sensible attitude seems to be: Whoever is most qualified should be in charge. But be sure the two of you agree in advance.

By the way, invite secretaries or typists to contribute their talent to your writing. Encourage them to suggest better ways of saying things. You will have better writing and better employee relations. But caution: Other people should not make changes without discussing the new wording with you first. If you were terribly unclear—and we are all sometimes—another person might misinterpret and say the wrong thing in trying to clarify.

Reviewing and Editing the Writing of Others

First, let us say that the subordinate's writing, like any other professional skill, is certainly the manager's business. But writing is more difficult to evaluate than most other job skills, because there is no quick or precise way to measure quality. And, because the writing in the office is so visible, many bosses have strong feelings about it and seem to become self-appointed experts. They may not always be right, and that can cause trouble. Some guidelines, therefore, are important.

In evaluating the writing of others, people often make one mistake: They assume that the best way to write anything is the way *they* would have written it. That is unwise and poor employee relations. There may be several equally good ways to write anything. **Even though the boss may be the better writer, it is unreasonable to expect that someone else should write a thing the way he or she would have written it.**

Another common mistake when dealing with other people's writing is to change things just for change's sake. For example, why change "A number of our representatives" to "Many of our representatives"? True, that change makes the writing a bit shorter, but is too minor a change to make *in other people's writing*. Again, it is poor employee relations, because it stifles initiative. Never give employees a chance to call you a nit-picker. How many times have we all heard people say, *"They're going to change everything anyhow, so what's the sense of trying to do a good job of writing?"* Sometimes that accusation is justified.

When reviewing someone else's writing, a wise attitude seems to be: "I am a watchdog, ensuring that what goes out meets our standards." A really wise watchdog should rejoice, however, if it is not necessary to bark.

Still, there are some things a reviewer has a right to expect. **Here is a six-point checklist for evaluating someone else's writing:**

- Is the content correct?
- Are the words clear?
- Are the ideas divided properly into sentences?
- Is the conclusion at the beginning?
- Is the tone courteous?
- Are there headings to help the reader?

If the answer to these questions is yes, the writing should pass. But what happens when you must honestly conclude that the writing is not good enough?

Many managers or reviewers rewrite it themselves. That is unwise, for two reasons. First, if it's poorly written the boss may misinterpret and say the wrong thing. Second, rewriting does not help the weak writer. If his or her work needs rewriting, the reviewer can help most by pointing out exactly what is wrong, and how to correct it. Are sentences too long? Words too complex? Is the organization weak? This kind of feedback is necessary if the subordinate is to improve. Both will benefit. The subordinate will learn to improve in an important professional skill, and the boss will need to spend less time editing and rewriting in the future.

Very minor editing and revising may not require discussion with the writer. But if changes are so extensive they reveal a basic writing deficiency, the manager should not correct the writing but teach the writer. That may be one of the greatest favors he or she can do.

Review of the outline. This is most useful for long reports, and we are surprised that many employers do not require it. Some people call this the "pre-editorial" review. Often a lot of work goes wasted because a writer learns *after* writing that the approach was not what the boss wanted.

Project directors, reviewers, or anyone else who has a voice in a report should approve the outline as well as the finished writing. Then, if they can help improve the overall approach, or want some other approach, the writer learns of it in advance. This saves a lot of rewriting. The finished writing then needs review only for editorial style—basic clarity. And that is exactly the way it should be.

The Trouble With Jargon

Jargon is the specialized vocabulary of a particular profession. When used legitimately, it is a kind of shorthand, allowing people in the profession to express complex ideas in a few words. But it has a major disadvantage: Only people in that profession can understand it.

Further trouble comes from the fact that jargon is also a status symbol; for this reason, professions often create specialized terms when none are necessary.

What does the doctor mean by *'topical'* dressings? Are they dressings related to a topic? Are they just *'top'* dressings? (Where else would they go?)

When lawyers discontinue a legal action, why do they say it has been *'continued'*? Why does the meaning of the term *'quiet enjoyment'* have nothing to do with either quiet or enjoyment? (It's a property term meaning *'uninterrupted use.'*) Lawyers argue that such phrases are "terms of art" and have specific meanings in court. But courts do not mandate their use. Plain English would be just as legal, and it would be more understandable to those of us who are governed by the laws.

It does not make sense to broadcast on a wavelength the person at the other end cannot receive—if you care to communicate.

Always remember, whether it is your writing or someone else's, that language is just a communications tool—a living tool of a living society. Your goal as a writer is to tell as much as possible, as clearly as possible, in as little reading as possible. That is the only purpose for which cultures create language. It is the only reason you write.

What Computers Can (and Can't) Do for Writers

They are the most significant technological development of our time, but can computers write for us? No, they cannot. Will they in the future? Not likely.

No computer manufacturers or program publishers are making such claims.

Computers can do some things that are helpful to writers. They can measure the size of words and sentences. They can warn if you use a word that's considered dangerous or commonly misused. And they can assemble letters—even large reports—from standard paragraphs held in storage; you just fill in the variable information. But someone has to write those standard paragraphs.

Some computer companies claim their systems can correct grammar and spelling. But that is far, far less than writing. *You* must still go through the same language process you have always gone through, to give the computer something it can correct. Then too, even those modest claims seem exaggerated. For example, a recently published best-selling book on personal computers stated (in its introduction) that its text had been edited by a well-known grammar program. Yet, the book contained occasional sentences in which subject and verb did not agree, or pronouns dangled. These are pretty basic errors; if computers can do no better, you should not count on them for much grammatical help in the near future.

What about spelling? Yes, inexpensive computer programs can warn you of misspelled words. Can you relax, then, smug with the confidence that you will never, ever again send out a letter with a typing error? Well, not really. Even in spelling, artificial intelligence has severe limitations. The computer warns you only if your misspelling, or other typing error, creates a non-word. If, for example you type *noj* instead of *now,* the display will call it to your attention, because *noj* is not on the program's approved word list. But if you type *not* instead of *now,* the computer will never blink an eye, because *not* is an approved word. That may reverse your meaning ('*Our company can not . . . .*' instead of '*Our company can now . . . .*'), but you will get no help from the electrons. It seems, then, for now anyhow, you will still have to proofread.

The real advantage computers offer writers is that revisions are so easy. The typist just replaces the words you change, and the printer gives you a new copy. Retyping the whole report is a thing of the past, and so is proofreading it again. As a result, writers can pamper themselves by making changes they might not have made in the past—second draft, third, tenth draft if they feel it is necessary—improvements they would not have made before because retyping would have been too much work.

Will computers ever write for us? If writing is one's thinking put on paper, a better way of asking that question might be: Will computers ever think for us?

Review

• •

How alert were you? All of these important points were discussed in the videotaped presentation you just watched. You should be able to answer them all. If you cannot, look them up in this book.

What three important benefits do subject headings give the reader in reports?

_____

_____

They also help you, the writer. How? _____

_____

What earlier aid should guide you in using headings? _____

How does it guide you? _____

Headings should stand out. If you cannot use heavy type, make them stand out by:

_____

_____

How wide should margins be? _____

Describe Mr. Joseph's advice on paragraph length.

_____

_____

If a report contains graphics, where should they generally appear?

_____

How can you add emphasis to written words and phrases, similar to the way you add emphasis by raising your voice when talking?

_____

When should you use each of these salutations in letters?

Dear (Name), _____

Dear Sir, _____

Gentlemen, _____

*What should one **not** expect when reviewing or editing the writing of others?*

_____

"Thinking is the process of simplifying the relationships between ideas. Therefore, simplicity is not only desirable— it is the mark of the thinking person."

—Albert Joseph